Managing the Corporate Media Center

Eugene Marlow

Knowledge Industry Publications, Inc.
White Plains, New York

Video Bookshelf

Managing the Corporate Media Center

Library of Congress Cataloging in Publication Data

Marlow, Eugene.
  Managing the corporate media center.

  (Video bookshelf)
  Bibliography: p.
  Includes index.
  1. Instructional materials centers—United States
  —Management. I. Title. II. Series
  Z674.5.U5M38   021.2   81-8155
  ISBN 0-914236-68-7   AACR2

Table of Contents

List of Tables and Figures

Foreword and Acknowledgements

The "media center" encompasses various media production activities: graphic arts, film production (in its various forms) and electronic media production (such as audio tape, video tape, and multimedia). The functions of media center-type operations are virtually universal to most organizations, regardless of how these functions are organized. However, as the last chapter argues, media production activities of today may not necessarily define the media center operations of tomorrow; particularly with the advent of such emerging technologies as teleconferencing and video discs.

Further, while most organizations engage in media production operations (using either internal resources, external resources, or a combination of the two), many organizations do not centralize their media production operations. It is this author's opinion that there are inherent relationships among the various communications media, and that, while many organizations evolve their media production functions in a hodge-podge manner, it does not have to be that way. The social and technological pressures of the 80s will preclude such an evolutionary process — which, in turn, will lead a lot more organizations to initiate, evolve and develop their media center operations in a more rational fashion.

The aim of this book is to assist managers and their organizations with both the development and the working realities of the corporate media center. It begins by looking at how and why a corporate media center is created, and then devotes individual chapters to examining the center's budget, organization and staffing. This is followed by discussion of how to solve communications problems, and a guide to the day-to-day operations of the center. The chapter on marketing the center (to top management, as well as to clients) applies some of the same communications techniques to the media center that are generally used by its clients. The chapter on working with executives, clients and content experts ought to be of interest to the entire center staff. We then look at the proper use of external resources, and end by discussing trends that we feel will particularly affect the evolving media center of tomorrow.

The appendices provide several comprehensive resource lists of readings in both media management; important professional organizations and publications, related educational institutions; and media competitions.

* * *

There are various people without whose guidance, expertise and assistance this volume could not have been written. I would like to acknowledge Barbara Lacher, who was primarily responsible for researching and organizing the listings in the appendices. Thanks, too, to Joanne Kaufman, who typed the original manuscript.

My thanks to Ellen Lazer, my editor at Knowledge Industry Publications, Inc., who first approached me with idea of the book and who brought clarity to my writing and ideas; and to Karen Sirabian, also at Knowledge Industry Publications, Inc., who handled the myriad of editing and production details that brought the manuscript to final book form.

Many thanks to Walter Baker and Bob McElree who created that rare environment at Union Carbide Corporation that allowed me to test and practice many of the principles outlined in this book; and to my staffs at Prudential Insurance and Union Carbide: together we learned how to do it better.

Most of all appreciation to my wife, Judy, for her constant support during the gratifying but often grueling task of putting one's thoughts and experiences on paper.

1

Creating the Corporate Media Center

Social and technological developments have expanded the scope and changed the complexity of corporate communications. Today corporate managers are faced with a multitude of communications problems that were either not considered problems 25 years ago or were far simpler: communications with government and regulatory bodies; with top executives, board members, stockholders and employees; with dealers and customers (increasingly on an international scale); with critics; with the press; even with other managers at corporate headquarters or locations halfway around the world.

The trend today towards demassification or "pluralism" continues to fragment our one-time "mass" society, creating even more complex communications problems for corporate managers. In addition, the many technological innovations of the last 25 years have involved communications devices that create greater access to more information by diverse publics: video tape, cable television, satellites, video discs, home computers — all communications technologies that allow for pluralistic communications environments.

These social and technological developments have had their effect on corporate communications activities. A cursory analysis of contemporary corporate America would show a vast array of employee and customer training activities; communications networks among far-flung and diverse corporate entities; ever-expanding techniques for employee communications; changing channels for marketing and sales communications; and new

methods for communicating with political, press and public groups. Furthermore, there are books, journals, newsletters, associations, seminars, and even academic degrees in communications subjects that were unimaginable twenty-five years ago!

THE EMERGING MEDIA CENTER

Paralleling this growth in the quantity and complexity of corporate communications activities has been the development of corporate media centers — organizational functions that generate various graphic, film, and electronic products for the purpose of solving a variety of organizational communications problems. Today's corporate media centers have sprung from, and continue to evolve in response to, the internal and external communications needs of America's corporations. The important point is that corporate media centers do not just happen — they develop in response to needs.

The last twenty-five years have shown that the communications needs of America's corporations have changed and will continue to change, and that the solutions to communications problems will also change. This chapter will show that the creation and development of a corporate media center that is properly organized, staffed, equipped and financed begins in response to the communications needs of the organization. Analysis of communications needs and media use then translates into a level of demand for media production resources. For many organizations, this leads to the creation, development and/or expansion of a media center. (See Figure 1.1.)

Figure 1.1: Overview: Determining the Need for a Corporate Media Center

Definition of Internal & External Communications Needs

↓

Definition of Media Needs (Graphic, Photographic/Cinemagraphic, Electronic)

↓

Media Production Resources Management

↓

Initiation and/or Development of the Media Center

COMMUNICATIONS ACTIVITIES

There are two broad areas of organizational communications activity: internal communications and external communications. A specific breakdown of these communications activities is given in Table 1.1.

Table 1.1: Internal and External Communications Activities

INTERNAL

Training

Role playing
Basic sales training
Dealer sales training/customer
   training (operations/service)
Product training
Technical training:
  Machine operation
  Maintenance and repair
  Trouble shooting
  Precision techniques
New procedures
Proficiency upgrading
Safety training
Operations improvement
Management development

Manufacturing

Quality control
Testing
Methods improvement
Documentation

Research & Development

Recording live tests
Communicating with marketing

General Employee Communications

Communications from
   headquarters to the field
Communications from
   the field to headquarters
Policy announcements
Marketing developments
Management conferences
Annual stockholders meetings
Orientation programs for new hires
Company benefits
Periodic news

EXTERNAL

Sales Promotion

Product demonstrations
New product introductions
Explanation of services
Sales trip reports
Sales meetings
Reports on competition

Marketing

Point of purchase
Trade shows
Reports on new applications
Reports on new markets
Testing new advertisements/
   promotion ideas
Communicating with
   research and development

Table 1.1: Internal and External Communications Activities (cont'd.)

External Communications

Recruiting new hires
Community relations
Government relations
Security analyst relations
Press conferences
Press relations
General public relations
Consumer relations
Visitor orientation programs
Visual facilities tours
Convention exhibits

DEFINING COMMUNICATIONS NEEDS

Organizations of any complexity are fraught with these internal and external communications activities and problems, many of which are served and solved by the appropriate use of various media. The initial problem for the organization as a whole is to uncover existing or potential communications needs and translate them into a level of demand for media production services: i.e., a media center.

Background Research

How and where can information about communications needs be obtained? The organization's annual report is a good place to start. It can provide an overview of the company's activities and growth patterns. Other source documents include organizational charts that provide information about reporting relationships, and recent press releases which will indicate major current organizational events.

The next step is to focus on divisions of the organization. Where are communications problems more likely to occur? Below we list a number of functions commonly found in most organizations. These are suggested starting points for the reader to investigate in terms of their levels of communication activity. Both background study and personal contact are recommended.

Organizational executives, such as the chairman of the board, the president, executive vice presidents and senior vice presidents.

Functional areas, such as accounting, auditing, building services,

5

community affairs, computer services, corporate contributions, controller's group, corporate accounting, corporate long range planning, corporate communications, employee relations, energy supplies and services, general services, government relations, health, safety and environmental affairs, human resources development, industrial relations, information systems planning, international affairs, investor relations, law, management development, medical, marketing services, office and information services, public affairs, purchasing, research and development, sales and marketing, secretarial, security, telecommunications, and university relations.

Operations management, such as division president, division vice presidents, product managers, national sales managers, regional sales managers, production managers, administrative systems managers, quality control managers, operations managers, plant managers, office managers and customer services managers.

Conducting Interviews

Fact-finding interviews can be immensely helpful in learning about the communications needs, activities and problems of the organization and its parts. Here are some typical questions one might ask during the interviews:

What are your most common communications activities?
What are your most common communications problems?
What medium or media do you currently use?
Which medium or media are the most dominant?
Do you find them effective?
How are they currently being produced?
Are there changes on the horizon that might necessitate changes in how and what you will communicate?
Will these communications activities increase in their level of activity or decrease?
How are internal and external communications currently distributed?

Organizing the communications patterns

The more interviews conducted, the more likely the conclusions will be validated. By the twentieth or thirtieth interview, a pattern will begin to emerge. As common communications problems and needs begin to make themselves known, they should be given top priority. After the fortieth—yes, or even the fiftieth interview!—one should have a very good overview of both the organization's operations and the communications problems either common to the entire organization or specific to parts of it. Every organization will be different. Some will exhibit many common communications problems across the board; others will exhibit problems that are specific to only one or more parts of the organization.

Figure 1.2 is a suggested matrix by which one can organize and analyze the information gleaned from the interviews.

Analyzing the data

Once the interviews are completed and first impressions have been reviewed, the next step is to cut the fat away from the meat. Some problems may seem trivial while more important ones may stand out if only because they have been referred to by many executives. Common, important issues might include the need for an overview of the organization's operations for orientation, community relations and recruiting. Or, it might be vital to concentrate on informing employees (especially middle managers) of laws or regulations requiring compliance (such as, environmental issues, business ethics or Securities and Exchange Commission regulations).

The responses might also be grouped according to which level the communications problem affects in the organization. Some communications have a corporate-wide audience, while others involve only a small, select portion of one division. Many communications problems fall somewhere between these two poles.

In order to facilitate the analysis, internal communictions activities can be ranked by audience in the following order:

•all employees throughout the organization
•all managers throughout the organization
•all hourly employees throughout the organization
•certain professionals throughout the organization
 (such as purchasing agents or quality control managers)
•certain specialists throughout the organization
 (such as keypunchers or word processing operators)

The same kind of structure can be applied to problems that concern only one division of the organization:

•all employees in the division
•all managers in the division

Figure 1.2: Communications Needs Analysis Matrix

Communications Need	Audience	Communications Frequency	Current Media	Means of Distribution
Internal communications				
Training				
Manufacturing				
R&D				
General employee communications				
Orientation				
Benefits				
External communications				
Sales promotion				
Marketing				
Recruiting				
Community relations				
Public relations				
Government relations				
Press relations				
Financial relations				

- all hourly employees in the division
- professionals in the division (such as purchasing agents or quality control managers
- certain specialists in the division
  (such as keypunchers or word processing operators)

External communications activities can also be ranked by audience, such as:

- customers
- recruitees
- community leaders
- local government leaders
- state government leaders
- federal government leaders
- international government leaders
- union leaders
- university and college leaders
- security analysts
- press corps
- other corporate executives
- stockholders
- professional associations
- trade groups
- consumer groups

Once the communications needs have been slotted into audience categories, one must then look at the immediacy of the problems: How many prospective clients need something done right away? How many can wait three to six months? How many do not need anything until next year? How many have a continuing need? The answers to these questions can then be put into three categories: short-term, intermediate-term and long-term.

Short-term refers to anything that must occur in a six to twelve month period; intermediate-term refers to anything that must happen within a one to three year period. Long-term refers to anything that must happen in a period over three years. Juxtaposing communications needs by content categories against the time factors should result in a solid overview of the organization's short to long range communications needs.

DEFINING THE MEDIA NEEDS

Before ultimately translating these communications activities (needs) and problems into an organizational media center, one must decide which media will be required. The various media under consideration in this book (see also Chapter 3, Organizing the Media Center) are:

- teleconferencing
- video disc
- multimedia
- video tape
- audio tape

- film
- slides
- still photography
- graphic arts
- print

Characteristics of Communications Media

Each medium has particular attributes which must be understood in order to effectively decide which to use for various situations. Table 1.2 summarizes some of the primary characteristics of the various media outlined above:

Table 1.2: Primary Characteristics of Communications Media

Medium	Primary Characteristics
Teleconferencing	Excellent for live, face-to-face meetings when travel/lodging expenses plus wear and tear on executives exceed cost of hardware installation and use expense over a three to five year period. Makes meetings more efficient and effective. Helps to increase managerial productivity.
Video disc	In high volume, duplication is less expensive than for video tape. Random access capability allows for a high degree of interaction. Excellent for training, general information communications and even sales promotion.
Multimedia	Can show various aspects of a single object, many objects or various time frames, simultaneously. Can use slides, film, video tape and audio, as well as "live" elements, simultaneously. Excellent for large audience viewings.

Table 1.2: Primary Characteristics of Communications Media (cont'd.)

Medium	Primary Characteristics
Video tape	Generally less expensive to produce and duplicate than film. Can use film, slides, multimedia, audio, still photography, graphic arts and print elements. Excellent for communicating content involving motor skills, and for attitude/behavior modeling. Communicates personality very well and provides immediate, live communications impact. It has immediate playback capability and is much faster to edit than film.
Audio tape	Relatively inexpensive to produce and distribute compared to video tape, film or slides. Can communicate information while the listener is focusing on other activities such as reading or even driving. Indispensable to video disc, video tape, film and multimedia production.
Film	Increasing film stock, editing and duplication costs make film less cost-effective, and therefore less viable. In certain cases, however, film is easier to use for production than video tape. Excellent for photoanimation. Good for large audience viewings, although the development of large screen video projectors may end this advantage. Useful when video players are not available.
Slides	Relatively inexpensive to produce, although price per slide may range from $15 to $150. Easily replaced when information becomes obsolete. Communicates facts effectively.
Still photography	Relatively inexpensive to originate. Does not require crews, as do video, film, multimedia and video disc productions. Relatively inexpensive capital investment required. Photography can be used in many other media, including teleconferencing, video disc, multimedia, video tape, film, slides and print.
Graphic arts	Indispensable media production activity to virtually every other communications medium.
Print	Enormous applicability. Used in conjunction with virtually every communications activity and medium. It is hard to imagine a communications activity without some print piece associated with it.

Choosing the Right Communications Media

There are various criteria for matching one medium (or media) with a communications activity:

- •communications frequency
- •audience size
- •audience location
- •communications content

Regarding communications frequency, if the communications content changes from day to day, or even from quarter to quarter, then media that are flexible, and have relatively quick production turnaround times should be used. On this basis, teleconferencing, audio and video tape, slides and print formats are most practical and effective. These media are effective for short-term communications activities primarily because of their ability to create the communications package quickly (ranging from teleconferencing which is inherently immediate to the other media mentioned above which take more time to create). Communications which will remain fairly unchanged over the long term may be served best by video disc, film and certain print products.

Audience size is a second criterion for choosing appropriate communications media. For large audiences, film, multimedia, video tape (using projection systems) and slides are most effective. For small audiences, virtually any medium can be used.

The location of the audience is another important factor. In small offices, for example, where there are no video tape players, a print piece may have to do the job.

The content of a communication will also help determine which medium is the most effective. Video tape is an excellent medium for role playing. Film and video tape are best for demonstrating motor skills. Electronic and film media are most suitable when content is highly visual in nature. Print media are best when content is primarily cognitive or factual in nature. Print media also allow the receiver an opportunity to review, study and analyze the communications content at a level of convenience not readily available with teleconferencing, multimedia or film. (More detailed discussion of "communications content" is found in Chapter 5, Solving Communications Problems.)

Based on the above, it can be seen that communications activities can benefit from selecting appropriate media by application (both individually and in conjunction with one another). Table 1.3 illustrates this further.

Table 1.3: Selecting Media by Application

Communications Activity	Potential Media

INTERNAL COMMUNICATIONS

General Employee Communications

Communications Activity	Potential Media
Annual stockholders meetings	Teleconferencing, video tape, film, slides, multimedia, print
Communications from field locations to headquarters	Video tape, print
Communications from headquarters to field locations	Video tape, film, print
Company benefits	Video disc, video tape, film, slides, print
Management conferences	Teleconferencing, video tape, film, slides, multimedia, print
Marketing developments	Video tape, slides, print
Medical information	Video disc, video tape, film, slides, print
Orientation program for new hires	Video disc, video tape, film, slides, print
Periodic news	Video tape, print
Policy announcements	Video print, print

Manufacturing

Communications Activity	Potential Media
Documentation	Video tape, film
Methods improvement	Video tape
Quality control	Video tape, print
Testing	Video tape

Research & Development

Communications Activity	Potential Media
Communicating to marketing	Teleconferencing, video tape, audio tape, slides, print
Recording of live tests	Video tape, film

Training

Communications Activity	Potential Media
Basic sales training	Video disc, video tape, audio tape, film, slides, multimedia, print
Dealer sales training/customer training (operations/service)	Video disc, video tape, film, slides, print
Management development	Video disc, video tape, audio tape, film slides, print
New procedures	Video disc, video tape, film, slides, print
Operations improvement	Video disc, video tape, film, slides, print
Product training	Video disc, video tape, film, slides, print

Table 1.3: Selecting Media by Application (cont'd.)

Communications Activity	Potential Media
Proficiency upgrading	Video disc, video tape, film, slides, print
Role playing	Video tape
Safety training	Video disc, video tape, film, slides, print
Technical training:	
Machine operation	Video disc, video tape, film, slides, print
Maintenance and repair	Video disc, video tape, film, slides, print
Trouble shooting	Video disc, video tape, film, slides, print
Precision techniques	Video disc, video tape, film, slides, print

EXTERNAL COMMUNICATIONS

General External Communications

Community relations	Video tape, film, slides, print
Consumer relations	Video tape, film, slides, print
General public relations	Video tape, film, slides, print
Government relations	Video tape, film, slides, print
Press conferences	Video tape, film, slides, print
Press relations	Video tape, film, slides, print
Recruiting	Video disc, video tape, film, slides, print
Security analyst relations	Video tape, film, slides, print
Visitor orientation programs	Video tape, film, slides, multimedia, print
Visual facilities tours	Video tape, film, slides, multimedia

Marketing

Communicating with research and development	Teleconferencing, video tape, audio tape, print
Point of purchase	Video disc, video tape, film, print
Report on new applications	Video tape, slides, print
Reports on new markets	Video tape, slides, print
Testing new advertisements/ promotion ideas	Video tape, film, print
Trade shows	Video disc, video tape, film, slides, multimedia, print

Table 1.3: Selecting Media by Application (cont'd.)

Communications Activity	Potential Media
Sales Promotion	
Explanation of services	Video disc, video tape, film, print
New product introductions	Video disc, video tape, film, print
Product demonstrations	Video disc, video tape, film, print
Reports on competition	Video tape, audio tape, slides, print
Sales trip reports	Video tape, audio tape, print
Sales meetings	Video tape, film, slides, multimedia, print

DEFINING MEDIA PRODUCTION RESOURCES

Thus far we have outlined how the organization can define its communications needs and give them a rank order in terms of (1) applicability to the organizational hierarchy, and (2) immediacy, and further, how those needs can be translated into the media required to support them. The next step is to uncover what resources, both internal and external, are now available to satisfy media production needs, and what will be needed in the future. In other words,

(1) Where are we now?
(2) Where do we want to go?
(3) How will we get there?

At this juncture the organization must translate into real terms media solutions to the organization's stated, perceived communications needs, be they training, marketing, sales, etc. These needs must then be discussed in terms of people, hardware, facilities and the operating budget. To accomplish this, each of the three questions asked above should be examined in more detail.

Assessing the Resources on Hand

Where are we now? What media production resources is the organization presently using to satisfy its current and immediate future media production needs? Questions to ask include:

How many people are on staff to produce video programs? films? multimedia productions?
How many photographers are on staff?

How many graphic artists are on staff?

How many video engineers and/or technicians are on staff?

What equipment (hardware) do we have in-house for video production? for film production? for multimedia production?

What equipment does the organization have in-house for slide and chart making?

What equipment does the organization have in-house for graphics production?

What facilities (space) does the organization have in-house for video production? film production? multimedia production?

What facilities does the organization have in-house for photography (such as adequate plumbing, electrical outlets, etc.)?

What facilities does the organization have in-house for graphics design and execution?

What is the current budget for video production? film production? multimedia production? photography production? slides and chart-making?

What use is the organization making of external resources in the areas of video, film, photography, slides and charting, and graphics arts? Who are the outside vendors?

What is the quality level of current in-house media production services?

What is the quality level of current external resources with respect to media production services?

What is the perception of organization executives with regard to in-house media production services?

What is the perception of organization executives with regard to external media production resources?

How are current in-house media production resources organized? Are they in one department? Two or more departments?

What is the current availability of teleconferencing facilities, video disc and video tape players, film projectors and slide projectors?

Figure 1.3 provides a suggested matrix for organizing the answers to these questions.

Determining Future Needs

Where do we want to go? This refers to where the organization sees itself in three to five years with respect to the use, organization, staffing,

Figure 1.3: Where Are We Now?

	Graphic Arts	Film	Electronic Media
Personnel (number):			
Equipment (type and value):			
Facilities (space, special requirements):			
Expense budget:			
Current applications (internal/external communications):			
Level of quality:			
How and where organized:			
Distribution systems:			
External resources used:			

equipping and budgeting of its media production functions — video, film, slides, multimedia, photography, graphic arts, teleconferencing, etc.

The answers to this question should reflect an analysis of the responses gleaned from the executive interviews. The overriding concept at this stage is that all future recommendations for staffing, equipping and budgeting grow out of the kinds of programs slated for production and the media that would be most effective for producing them. Once the short-to-long range software needs have been determined, these applications can be translated into people: for example, how many video producers will be needed in the next six to twelve months? in the next one to two years? in the next three to five years? The same can be asked for photographers, graphic artists, video engineers, slide and charting specialists, etc.

Based on the answers given one can begin to determine equipment needs: What type of video production and post-production equipment is necessary? How many still cameras are needed? How many cameras for slide production? What kind of lighting instruments? What type of audio tape and multimedia production equipment?

The amount of personnel and equipment necessary will in turn determine the facilities needed: How much space will be required? How much heating, ventilating and air conditioning (known as HVAC)? Any special requirements regarding acoustics, plumbing, electricity, ceiling height, storage, color, lighting, meeting rooms, screening rooms, library, workrooms, maintenance room? How many office spaces will be needed.

Further, what is the need for distribution equipment, such as video disc and video tape players, film and slide projectors, teleconferencing facilities? What kinds of changes will be needed?

Figure 1.4: How Do We Get There?

	YEAR I	YEAR II	YEAR III	YEAR IV-V
Volume of production				
Graphic arts				
Still photography				
Slides				
Cinematography				
Audio tape				
Video tape				
Multimedia				
Video disc				
Teleconferencing				
Number of personnel				
Graphic arts				
Film				
Electronic media				
Equipment budget				
Graphic arts				
Film				
Electronic media				
Facilities				
Graphic arts				
Film				
Electronic media				
Expense budget				
Graphic arts				
Film				
Electronic media				

Plotting the Course of Action

How will we get there? This question is essentially one of timing, i.e., not if, but when. By now the organization has determined what action must be taken (e.g., hiring staff, purchasing equipment, etc.) in order to meet its long-term communications goals. What remains is to integrate the organization's long term media production needs with the realistic short-to-intermediate term budget constraints, and, perhaps ever more so, with management's perception of what is important. Figure 1.4 suggests a way to organize this information (please also refer to Chapter 2, Budgets).

DEVELOPING A STRATEGY

There are several reasons for having an internal media center operation; namely accessibility, geographical convenience and maintaining the security and confidentiality of proprietary information. An organization may need weekly or even daily access to media production personnel and facilities. Second, the organization may be too far from a metropolitan center with readily available external resources. Finally, an organization may decide to provide for an in-house media production operation if only to control the security of proprietary information.

The Economics of Internal and External Media Production

Much of the "when" decision to initiate, expand, modify or even contract media production operations is based on volume, which is another way of saying economics. Taking video as an example, if an organization produces 15 or less programs a year, it is probably economically better off using outside resources. If the company is producing 15 to 35 programs a year, it could consider buying production equipment, but using outside facilities for editing. Last, if the company is producing 35 to 50 or more programs a year, it may be more cost-effective to have both production and post-production capabilities in-house. (Of course, these figures are somewhat arbitrary; moreover, they are irrelevant if external facilities are not accessible.) Also it should be remembered that having an in-house facility does not exclude the use of external resources, the topic of Chapter 9.

A company does not necessarily save money merely by buying and owning equipment. A 1-inch video tape recorder or Forox slide camera does not cost the organization less than it costs an outside facility. It is through the people a company hires to use the equipment that savings can be achieved.

Generally speaking, the ratio of internal to external aggregate costs is frequently 1:2. In other words, what costs fifty cents to produce in-house often costs one dollar to produce externally. In certain instances, savings are achieved by owning the equipment (particularly AV equipment — 16 mm film and 35mm slide projectors — that may be loaned to users within other departments of the organization.) When it comes to video, film, multimedia and photography production, however, it is clear that the real savings are created by using on-staff personnel, as opposed to contracting exclusively with outside personnel. From my experience I have concluded that having the people in-house to manage media production can reduce production expenses from 25% to 50%, as compared to turning the job over entirely to an outside company. However, the economics will vary from region to region and company to company.

The development of an in-house media operation, therefore, could well occur over a period of years. In the short term, a strategy may call for the initial hiring of a media manager and later, in-house producer/directors who use outside production (hardware) facilities. Over the next one to two year period, as volume grows, the economics may demand the purchase of equipment and hiring of technicians. If the volume of production grows, the purchase of additional equipment may be warranted. Increased volume may also herald the need for additional producer/directors and administrative support personnel.

The central factor here is volume: one to three films a year does not warrant the development of an in-house cinemagraphic unit. Twelve to fifteen video programs a year does not warrant the creation of an in-house group (except under extreme circumstances). The need for a photographer or graphic artist two to three days a month does not support the need for a full-time, in-house photographic or graphic arts operation.

A way of looking at the "economic timetable" factor is to take each aspect of the media center operation and compare its internal cost to its external cost. One can then judge when it becomes economical to hire personnel purchase equipment and/or expand the operating expense budget.

Let's look at two examples. A staff photographer is hired at an annual salary of $20,000 (including benefits). If an outside photographer charges $250 per day plus expenses (a low figure in some parts of the country), then the staff photographer is highly cost-effective. Presuming there are 250 working days in the year and the organization has enough volume of work for a photographer every working day, then an outside photographer would cost the organization $62,500 a year! Conversely, if an organization only has a need for a photographer 80 days out of the year, then an outside photographer would prove more cost-effective (80 days x $250 = $20,000 a year).

On the equipment side, presume an organization is considering the purchase of a $40,000 video camera. Also figure that it costs this particular organization $1000 a day to rent a video camera, including a technician and a professional cameraman. If this organization is producing 20 programs a year, the economic payback of purchasing the camera is two years. Purchase of the camera, of course, may lead to the increased use of video as a communications medium, which would result in a faster payback on the capital investment.

In effect, the organization must make an economic judgment about (1) staff requirements, (2) capital equipment requirements and (3) concomitant operating budget expenses for each communications medium perceived as needed by the organization. Again, the overriding criterion is volume. When the production activity gets high enough (depending on the medium in question and relative external costs), it is time to hire personnel, purchase equipment, expand the operating budget or do all three simultaneously.

One other issue remains: the quality of the people and equipment required. In my experience two principles have proven most practical, effective and efficient: good people produce quality work, and the proper equipment does the right job.

The Media Center Development Process

In all, presuming it takes an average of four or five years from initiation of an in-house media production operation to maturity, the step-by-step process might resemble the one illustrated in Table 1.4.

Table 1.4: Chronological Development of a Media Center Production Operation

Year I	Needs analysis — performed either solely by in-house personnel or in conjunction with outside consultants familiar with communications needs analysis techniques, media production and long range planning.
	Develop short and long range plans.
	Organization designates individual to coordinate media production operations.
	Organization makes extensive use of external resources.

Table 1.4: Chronological Development of a Media Center Production Operation (cont'd.)

Year II	As volume increases, organization hires production personnel: graphic artists, photographers, video/film/multimedia producers, as required.
	Essential hardware purchased. External resources continue to be used (unless unavailable for geographical reasons).
Year III	As volume continues to grow, more hardware purchased and additional staff hired, particularly technical personnel.
Year IV to V	Additional software personnel hired. External resources continue to be used.

For an organization that has an existing media production operation, a year to year analysis might provide evidence that a re-organization of media production functions is warranted, or that some part of the operation should be expanded, or others contracted. Such analyses should be performed routinely by media center management, as well as by higher management. Figures 1.3 and 1.4, referred to earlier, provide suggested matrices to use for these types of analyses.

In sum, the order of events in the media center development process is (1) analysis, (2) short and long range plans, (3) hiring of people, (4) purchase of equipment and, as volume grows, (5) the appropriate proportions of additional equipment and personnel — in that order!

THE PLAN

Funds. Money. Capital. Dollars. Eventually, all the research, analysis, structuring, looking at the present, the future and ways of getting to the future boil down to a dollar figure: a year-by-year budget projection. (See Chapter 2 for a more detailed discussion of budgets.) Let us assume for the moment, however, that budgets have been developed. The final step in this evaluation process is the preparation of a plan.

First, plans should be direct and clear. Second, they should be succinct. Third, they should be thorough. Fourth, they should be cogent.

The plan should have several content elements. The opening should contain a short introduction to the scope and purpose of the plan, sometimes called an "Executive Summary." The next section should follow the structure discussed earlier, namely: where are we now? where do we want to go? how do we get there? This section should be an explication of the current state of media production affairs, followed by a projection of where the organization should be in three to five years, concluding with how the organization should develop media production resources in that time period.

Other sections of the proposal could include a survey on the use of media in other organizations, especially those within the organization's industry. One might also include a chart showing cost comparisons between maintaining the use of outside resources, for example, versus developing an in-house resource (with thoroughly researched outside costs). Such a chart should cover at least a five year period. Items such as software costs (producer/directors, writers) should be shown, along with costs for hardware purchased. Maintenance as well as overhead costs should also be included in the cost analysis. Projected production volume growth-curves should also be indicated; that is, at what point does the cost of in-house production become more economical (as well as convenient) to the organization, than the exclusive use of outside resources?

Finally, one might also include, in an appendix, the list of organizational executives interviewed, and the analysis of the primary communications problems articulated. It is, after all, this information that has led to the conclusions that form the basis of the plan.

The quantification of facts based on thorough research, and presented in a succinct manner, is more helpful than a barrage of words. Organizational media production is not entertainment but business, and must reflect a direct relationship between use and economic impact. For an organizational media center to be successful it must accomplish the following task: the effective and efficient production of media that communicates information effectively and efficiently. Finally, the success of an organizational media center, from an economic point of view, is developing a cost-effective in-house media operation, and producing media programming that provides positive economic results for the organization.

2

Budgets

At the heart of every successful media center is a well-planned, well coordinated and well-controlled budget. Without one, the organizational media center is a mere appendage on the side of the organizational body without a defined function or realizable benefit. With a properly structured annual budget, the media center can flourish and provide management with proof that it is making a contribution to the organization.

The development of an annual budget must be a direct outgrowth of the needs analysis, as discussed in the previous chapter. In this sense, the development of the budget is a matter of economic analysis, frequently defined as the optimal use of scarce resources to satisfy human wants. In the case of media center operations, human wants include the need to communicate information effectively and efficiently. Scarce resources include capital and operating dollars to staff, equip and provide operating monies to support communications activities. The optimal use of these scarce resources is what this book is about.

THE BUDGET'S FUNCTION

The budget can be defined as having three functions: (1) planning future operations; (2) coordinating the organization's activities; and (3) controlling the action of employees.[1] For the corporate media center, a good budget system provides planning by determining: the demand for media

25

1982 • budgets • graphic arts • reason for purchase • equipment • cost • payback period • item • salaries •non-capital equipment • conferences • 1st quarter • printing • office supplies • video production • operating budget • travel • price • telephone (local) • production expenses • duplication services • 2nd quarter • mailing costs • payroll taxes • overtime • teleconferencing • capital equipment budget • multimedia • books, pamphlets • travel • maintenance • repair • 3rd quarter • data processing • word processing • per diem expenses • video production • fiscal year • reclamation of errors • rent • billings • 4th quarter • audio equipment • telephone (long distance) • benefit plans • materials • building services • consultants • cinemagraphic • photographic • shared expenses • annual budget • 1982 • budgets • graphic arts • reason for purchase • equipment • cost • payback period • item • salaries •non-capital equipment • conferences • 1st quarter • quarter • audio equipment • telephone (long distance) • benefit plans • materials • building services • consultants • cinemagraphic • photographic • shared expenses • annual budget • maintenance • repair • 3rd quarter • production expenses • duplication services • 2nd quarter • mailing costs • payroll taxes • overtime • teleconferencing • capital equipment budget • multimedia • data processing •

production services; the expected cost of providing those services; the amount and cost of equipment required; and the operating expenses required. Control of the operation is achieved by means of periodic reports (either monthly, quarterly or semi-annually) for each part of the media center. These budgetary performance reports reflect the budget amounts for each activity against the real expenditures.

Planning Future Operations

A periodic review of these budgets gives management an opportunity to investigate major differences between budget and actual performance. It also allows management to ascertain why predetermined plans have or have not been met and, in the latter case, to consider alternative courses of action. The budget may be thought of as a formal, written statement of management's plans for the future, expressed in financial terms. A budget charts the course of future action. It serves management in the same manner the architect's blueprints assist the builder. Like a blueprint, a budget should contain attainable objectives rather than mere wishful thinking.

A budget encourages planning because careful study, investigations and research must be given to expected future operations if the budget is to contain sound, viable goals. Advanced planning, in turn, increases the reliance of management on fact-finding in making decisions and lessens the role of hunches and intuition in managing the operation.

Organizational Coordination and Control

Coordination is facilitated as each level of management in the media operation participates in the preparation of the budget. In addition, a budget enables higher management to explain its objectives to each stratum in the organization and to keep these goals before the entire organization. As a result, employees within the operation are more integrated. Budgeting also contributes to effective control through the preparation of periodic budget reports. Finally, budget objectives also serve to encourage effectiveness and efficiency, cost savings, and have the potential for serving as a deterrent against waste.[2]

THE PARTS OF A BUDGET

The model for developing a media center budget is no different than one for any other aspect of an organization. Speaking in marketing terms, the manager of the in-house media operation should adopt the attitude that his or her operation is an in-house "agency," in competition with any other "media agency" in the organization and any and all externally based media production operations. Thus the need for a proper, business-like budget becomes even more obvious. As we proceed through the various steps and aspects of developing a media center budget, keep in mind that this budget is a business budget.

For planning, coordinating and control purposes, we must really deal with two types of budgets: an operating budget, and a capital budget. The operating budget refers to expenses incurred during the fiscal year. The capital budget, on the other hand, refers to the purchase of equipment or facilities usually of value over $500. The primary reason for separating these two kinds of budgets is that operating expenses will usually occur and be paid for in that year. Capital expenditures, however, refer to things like buildings and equipment — items which have a life of more than one year. Obviously, video tape equipment, cameras, lighting equipment, animation stands, audio recording equipment and photographic processing equipment have a life of more than one year, and therefore, should be considered separately from the operating budget. Use Figure 2.1 as a suggested format for developing the annual operating expense budget, and Figure 2.2 for the capital equipment budget.

The Operating Budget

For purposes of convenience, the operating budget can be divided into various sections:

    (1) Employee Expenses
    (2) Direct Expenses
    (3) Shared Expenses
    (4) Billings

Employee expenses

Employee expenses can be subdivided as follows: employee salaries; overtime expense; benefits plans expenses; and employee payroll taxes. These are relatively self-explanatory expenses.

Direct expenses

Direct expenses may include a whole host of items, such as: materials and supplies; printing, stationery and office supplies; maintenance and repair expenses; travel expenses; external resources.

Figure 2.1: The Operating Expense Budget

Item	1st Quarter* Actual/Budget	•••	Annual Actual/Budget
Salaries			
Overtime			
Benefit Plans Expense			
Payroll Taxes			
Materials/Suppliers			
Printing, Stationery and Office Supplies			
Maintenance & Repair			
Travel			
Non-Capital Equipment			
Books, Pamphlets, Periodicals			
Conferences and Conventions			
Staff Training			
Telephone (Local)			
Telephone (Long Distance)			
Internal Maintenance			
Building Services			
Shared Administrative			
Duplication Services			
Mail			
Word Processing			
Data Processing			
Consultants			
Production Expenses:			
Writers			
Per Diem Producers			
Per Diem Directors			
External Production			
External Post Production			
Per Diem Freelancers			
Canned Materials			

*Format would be repeated for 2nd Quarter, 3rd Quarter, etc.

Figure 2.2: The Capital Equipment Budget

Item	Cost	Reason For Purchase	Payback Period
Graphic Arts			
Photographic (Still & Slides)			
Cinemagraphic			
Video Production			
Audio Production			
Multimedia			
Video Disc			
Teleconferencing			

One might also want to include a budget line here for non-capital equipment expenditures (items that cost less than $500); the demarcation line may differ from organization to organization.

Another group of direct expenses falls into the general area of professional development, such as: books, pamphlets and periodicals; conferences and conventions; and staff training.

A budget amount for the purchase of outside services, such as temporary office help might also be included. Some organizations include a budget line for covering errors incurred by the operation. For example, say the slide making department makes a mistake producing a program and the work has to be redone. The cost of that mistake would be placed in the "reclamation of errors" budget line.

Shared expenses

Shared or "overhead" expenses would include such things as: telephone; rent; internal maintenance and repair; building services (such as cleaning); shared administration expenses; use of internal duplication services; use of internal mail services; and use of internal word processing services.

Some organizations' media centers might consider paying for their share of the amount of electricity (for electronic equipment, for example) and water used (for the photography department, for instance).

Billings

The last item on the operating budget — Billings — is the bottom line, so to speak. It is this item which will determine how profitable or unprofitable the organizational media center operation is. The total annual amount of billings will depend, of course, on a variety of factors. Among these are the rate card developed for the media center (see also Chapter 6), and the volume of work. Billings, then, refers to the amount of money (sometimes referred to as "funny money") charged to internal clients for media center services.

If billings exceed the total of employee salaries, direct expenses and shared expenses, then the organization is running a profitable media center. If the billings more or less equal the total of employee salaries, direct and shared expenses, the operation is break-even. However, if media center billings run short of the total of all expenses, then the organization is, to a certain degree, carrying the media center as excess overhead. In some organizations the excess is divided equally or divided according to a pre-set formula among all operating divisions.

The long term survival of the media center depends, of course, on a variety of factors. But one of the more important factors is the parity between expenses and billings. At the very least, a break-even operation is one that shows that the media center is paying for itself; that there is demand for its services; and that internal clients want those services and are willing to pay a price for them.

The Capital Budget

A capital budget represents all the hardware a media center might require, ranging from special filing systems for graphics, to video cameras and computer editing systems.

The equipment to be itemized might include:

- audio recording and mixing equipment
- cinemagraphic equipment
- distribution amplifiers
- film audio recorders
- film projectors
- graphic design tables
- graphic storage
- lighting instruments
- multimedia programmers
- photographic processing
- slide duplication cameras
- slide productions stands
- still photography cameras
- 35mm slide projectors
- video cameras
- video editors
- video tape recorders

The capital equipment budget might also take into account the media center facility itself. For instance, the photo lab will have special requirements for water and chemical drainage. The video operation might have special requirements for studio ceiling heights, air conditioning and perhaps computer flooring in editing rooms. The graphic arts group may have demands for special lighting. Heating, ventiliating and air conditioning requirements (HVAC) may also have to be customized, especially in the electronic part of the center. All of these aspects need to be worked out and developed within the capital equipment budget.

DEVELOPING A BUDGET

The development of an annual budget for an ongoing media center is easier than developing a budget for a new one, primarily because an ongoing operation has a history; year to year comparisons can be made, percentage increases in budgets (or decreases, if necessary) can be more easily justified, etc.

Employee Expenditures

So let us talk for the moment about developing a budget for a brand new media center, starting with employee salaries. The amount of employee salaries will depend, of course, on the result of the needs survey, as was discussed in Chapter 1. These kinds of questions will have been answered: How many producer/directors will be needed? How many photographers? How many graphics artists? How many video engineers and/or technicians? To a degree the salary level of each of these production professionals will be determined by various factors: the supply of qualified professionals in the area; the specific region of the country where the organization is located; the general level of salaries for qualified professionals in the country; negotiations between prospective employees and the organization; and the general salary structure of the organization.

Expenses for employee benefits plans and payroll taxes will probably be the easiest budget items to determine, primarily because the organization should have already developed formulas for determining these. The formulas will vary depending on the kind of organization, and the state and locality in which the organization is situated.

Determining Direct Expenses

A certain amount of guesswork will be made with respect to direct expenses, especially if the organization has no previous media production history. For example, let's take materials and supplies. In this budget item you might want to include video tape stock, photographic paper and processing materials, slide mounts and 35mm film, paper, ink, audio tape stock, bulbs, and so on. Again, the amount of materials needed in this area will be an outgrowth of the needs analysis performed earlier. One source of information for determining these particular budget items is an outside professional in the business. During the early stages of developing an organizational media production operation, the organization might consider hiring a consultant to help put together the first year's budget. (Consultants are discussed further in Chapter 9).

On the other hand, professional development expenses should be fairly easy to determine. Relevant trade periodicals and associations are listed in Appendices II and III. A rundown of the ones that would be appropriate for your organization along with a few phone calls should quickly determine how much you will need for periodicals, conferences and employee professional development.

Determining Shared Expenses

Administrative history can be a guide with respect to shared expenses. Telecommunications management should be able to determine the yearly telephone expenses, depending on how many personnel will be in the department for the year, how many will have one or two lines, how much long distance telephone calling can be expected and so on. Rent should also be a rather simple matter. Presuming the organization has determined a square footage rate for rent, once facility requirements (both office and production) have been established, it should be a simple matter of determining how much will have to be budgeted for rent. Internal maintenance and repair work may require some guesswork but in the overall context of the larger budget, a 10% miss here would not be devastating. One can determine a reasonable amount for this budget item by inquiring what internal maintenance and repair work rates are. Cleaning services can be determined likewise. Shared administrative expenses may be dictated by the needs and wants of higher management. Last, internal duplication, mail and word processing services expenses can be determined by finding out what the rates are and estimating the usage of these internal services.

Researching Other Sources

Prices for staff, hardware and direct expenses change from time to time, and differ depending on what part of the country the organization is in. Thus, while experience may be a good starting point for the determination of both the operating and capital equipment budgets, there are various sources one can research in order to get an idea of prices for such items as consultants, production facilities, production houses, freelancers, hardware vendors and suppliers.

Trade publications are a good source for finding people to talk to regarding prices. They often publish lists of facilities or hardware with the latest list prices. Professional organizations might be useful for determining the range of salaries for certain professional positions. Occasionally, a professional organization will publish a salary survey. The International Television Association (ITVA), for example, publishes an annual Salary Survey. Media center managers at other companies nearby might also be helpful in getting a handle on what prices should be. Hardware companies provide press releases, brochures, catalogs and other information about their products.

THE EVOLVING BUDGET

The dollar size of the budget will depend upon the kind of organization the media production operation is in, the size of the staff, the size of equipment and facilities required and the volume of work. Moreover, the budget should be ready to accommodate ad hoc decisions that might be required during the course of a year that will enable media center management to expand (or modify) activities without having to go to higher management to make changes.

A well prepared budget that is both complete and flexible will give media center management the ability needed to make decisions more independently of higher management. To repeat, a budget is not an instrument of dictatorship; it is, rather, a tool for management to plan, coordinate and control. Management will expect the media center manager to use his or her budget judiciously. This may mean the manager will have to make decisions during the year that go beyond the original intent of the budget, but still remain within the larger scope of the media center's operations. Therefore, monthly or even quarterly budget reports on how much has been spent and how much has been charged to clients is an ideal time frame within which media management can track the progress of the center.

In the final analysis, while a media center operation may receive dozens of awards and be considered effective and efficient, the survival of the operation depends largely on economic factors: does it make a profit, does it break even or does it cost the organization money? From the outset, it should be the goal of the media center manager to develop a break-even operation. At a break-even point there can be very little argument: the media center is paying for itself, ergo, it has value to its users. However, organizational management may take the position that for at least the first year or two, these services can be provided freely to organizational clients until some history can be developed, expenses determined and the volume of potential business takes shape. Once this phase has been passed, there is no reason why an organization should not start charging for media services. While this will not hold for every organization, it seems that the more services media centers charge for, and the higher they charge, the greater the esteem media centers are held in, and the greater their volume of work gets. Perhaps it is the nature of business. Charging for services seems to add a higher value to these services than offering them for free. In the long term, organizations should be charging full-fare for media center production services, and the rate of the charge should be whatever the market will bear. (The rate of charges will be discussed in Chapter 6, Day to Day Operations.)

FOOTNOTES

1. Robert E. Seiler, *Elementary Accounting: Theory, Technique, and Applications* (Columbus, OH: Charles E. Merrill Publishing Co, 1969), p.635.

2. A good text on this subject is: Howard S. Noble and C. Rollin Niswonger, *Accounting Principles* (Cincinnati,OH: South-Western Publishing Co., 1961), pp.621-22.

3

Organizing the Media Center

The proper organization of a corporate media center can be just as important to its effectiveness as a well-planned budget. The central questions to focus on regarding the organization of media production functions are:

(1) What activities define media production functions?
(2) Which media production functions belong together in the media center?
(3) Where in the organization does the media center as a whole belong?

DEFINING MEDIA PRODUCTION

We have already mentioned the media production operations that define the organization's media functions, namely:

- teleconferencing
- video disc production
- multimedia production
- video production
- audio production

- film production
- slide production
- still photography
- graphic arts
- print*

---

*In the context of this book, printing or print duplication, is perceived as an administrative function, rather than a media center production function.

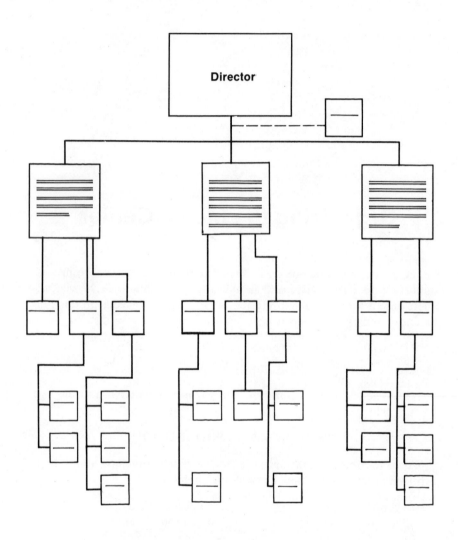

The media mentioned above reflect the various technologies man has developed for communications: speech, written symbols, printing, still photography, film and slides, broadcast television and multimedia. Video disc and teleconferencing are emerging technologies.

Looking at an organization's use of communications media is like looking at a cross section of the Grand Canyon: there are many layers, and the older ones have been around for many years. They have not disappeared, they are still serving a function. In a manner of speaking, they support the newer layers (in this context, the newer technologies).

New technologies are additive; they seem to have the ability to use the characteristics of older technologies. For example, written symbols (such as the alphabet) are representations of speech; the content of printing is written symbols; the content of photography is graphic renderings (painting, for example); the content of film is still photography (film is a series of still frames — photographs — moving at 24 frames a second); the content of electronic communications (such as radio, audio tape, television and video tape) is all the other previously mentioned media. You can put a photograph, slide or film into television (but you cannot put a television program into a film, slide or photograph). Multimedia by definition implies that it uses all the other media. The current major differences between electronic media and multimedia presentations are of scale, portability and accessibility. Not everyone can communicate via a multimedia presentation; a television presentation is accessible to a lot more people. The video disc likewise can absorb all the communications characteristics of speech (audio), print, photography, film, television and multimedia. The video disc also allows the user an effective random access, "interactive" feature not typical of other media.

Inter-Relationships Among Production Functions

It would be impossible for the various organizational media production functions to operate totally independently. Sooner or later one production function will use or work with another. The frequency of the inter-relationship will depend on the nature of the organization, the expertise of those involved in media production, the availability of sophisticated hardware and, finally, the manner in which media production functions are organized.

For example, a house organ editor may regularly require the services of the graphics arts group for layout and design, as well as the still photography group for originating and developing still photographs. A manager in need of a slide presentation requires the services of the slide production group, as well as the graphic arts department, for preparing the mechanicals to later be presented in slide format. If a manager wants to produce a film, he or she will require the services of a producer/director, as well as the expertise of cinemaphotographers from the photography unit; the slide group may also get involved if photo animation sequences (using slides as the raw material) are required; and the graphic arts group may also be needed if titles or storyboards have to be prepared.

A video production may require the services of all other media production functions, including engineering and technical support; a producer/director; a still photographer for the origination of slides and/or photographs; a cinemaphotographer for the creation of film footage; a graphic artist for the design and execution of titles and storyboards (even set design), and the audio production unit (for the creation of sound tracks involving music-mixed/voiceover and music sound effects tracks). A multimedia production would likewise require the services of all media production groups for obvious reasons.

The more advanced the technology, or the more recent the communications technology required, the more complex the execution of that communication becomes, thus requiring the services of more parts of the media production operation.

Interface of Production and Presentation Modes

Table 3.1 illustrates how the mode of production interfaces with the mode of presentation. As you will note, the more traditional communications media (graphic arts, photography, slides) have a higher degree of interface with the other presentation media, as opposed to the newer media of film, video and multimedia. Graphic arts is the one media production origination group that interacts with all the other presentational media.

THE STRUCTURE OF MEDIA PRODUCTION OPERATIONS

The various media production operations fall into three groups: electronic media, film and graphic arts:

(1) Teleconferencing, video disc, multimedia, video and audio production can be considered one group, electronic media, since electronics is at the heart of these communications presentations.
(2) Cinematography, slides and still photography belong in the film group primarily because film in various formats (super 8mm, 16mm, 35mm transparency and still photography) is the technological heart of the activity.

(3) Graphic arts and printing become a third group, primarily because these functions are print oriented.

Several organizational elements remain to be considered: management; the differentiation between software professionals (producer/directors) and hardware professionals (engineers and technicians); and the administrative element.

The question of management is straightforward. Adding this necessary element to the three just discussed results in a basic organizational chart such as the one illustrated in Figure 3.1.

Figure 3.1: Basic Organizational Chart

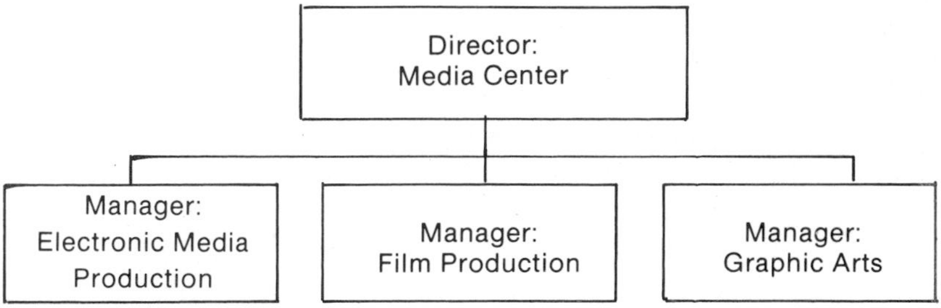

Differentiation Between Software and Hardware Professionals

Within each group is the need for a differentiation between software and hardware professionals. For example, a video producer/director is a software professional while a video engineer is a hardware professional. Graphic artists, too, can be considered software professionals. However, photographers (whether for film, slides or stills) present a bit of a problem; those involved in originating the production elements of photographic (film) media are both software and hardware professionals. In the case of 35mm slides and still photography, the photographer is often conceptualizer, originator and finisher. However, in motion photography a bit more is involved. A film requires producer/director talent and skill not only for successful production origination, but also for production completion and distribution. Thus, in the case of film, an organizational cinematographer may work with an organizational producer/director, plus a host of external software and hardware experts, such as film editors and film processing labs.

Table 3.1: Production/Presentation Interactions

Production Origination	Presentation Mode								
	Telecon-ferencing	Video Disc	Multi-media	Video	Audio	Film	Slides	Photo-graphy	Graphic Arts
Teleconferencing	X								
Video disc	X	X							
Multimedia	X	X	X	X		X			
Video	X	X	X	X		X			
Audio	X	X	X	X	X	X			
Film	X	X	X	X		X			
Slides	X	X	X	X		X	X		
Photography	X	X	X			X	X	X	
Graphics arts	X	X	X	X		X	X	X	X

A producer/director is necessary for the development of a film, audio tape, video production, multimedia presentation, video disc or teleconference. The development of a slide presentation, still photography elements or a graphic presentation may not necessarily require the coordination of a producer/director. Whereas in graphics the graphic artist can be both the designer and executer of the presentational element, the execution of a professional video program cannot be carried out by one person.

Thus, if producer/directors are to be effective in the media production organization, they should be placed where the highest level of media coordination is likely to occur: in electronic media production. Because this group will also require the heaviest investment in hardware and facilities, the hardware professionals required should also be put in this group.

There is also a natural split in photography, between slides (if for no other reason than sheer volume), and still photography and cinematography. Figure 3.2 depicts the organizational chart as it now looks.

The Administrative Function

Within the media center structure, one last group is needed for such activities as billing, processing invoices, tracking costs, providing audiovisual equipment loan services and conference room set-ups, meetings services, media distribution and media library services. Thus, an administrative group is formed to round out the centralized media center structure. The completed organizational chart for the media center is shown in Figure 3.3.

A centralized approach to the organization of corporate media activities (such as the one given in Figure 3.3, referred to previously) seems to be the best one to take. This is supported by the results of a survey of fifty United States and eastern Canadian companies I conducted several years ago.[1] The survey intended to assess where and how nine "communications functions" were organized. The functions were: (1) video production; (2) printing; (3) graphic arts/photography/AV production; (4) training; (5) press relations; (6) government relations; (7) employee communications, (benefits information and house organs); (8) advertising; and (9) community relations. A second purpose was to ascertain if there was an ideal model for the organization of communications functions. Those responding to the survey strongly indicated that the "ideal" model for the greatest efficiency and effectiveness of communications functions was a well centralized model. Two findings of interest are:

(1) Printing production was seen by 65% of those surveyed as a function of administration, rather than of communications.

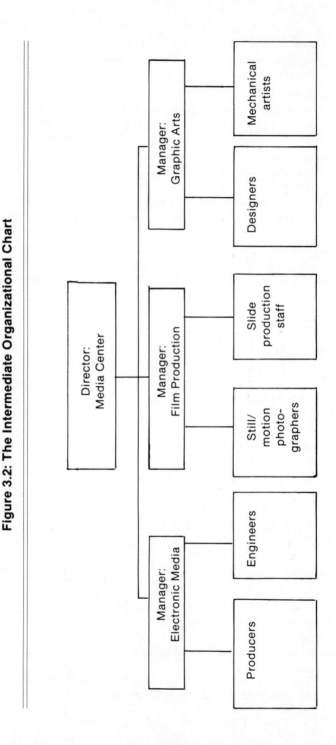

Figure 3.2: The Intermediate Organizational Chart

Figure 3.3: Organization of the Media Center

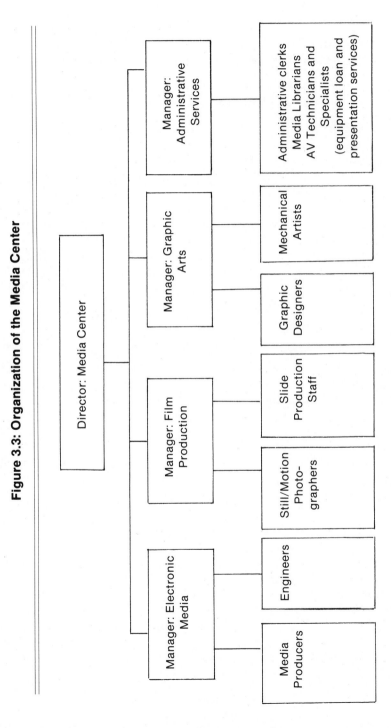

(2) The video and graphics functions were organized into the same department in 60% of the corporations perceiving their model of communications functions as the ideal model, or close to it.

WHERE THE MEDIA CENTER BELONGS
WITHIN THE ORGANIZATION

One of the most important decisions to make concerning the media center, is where it will be placed in the overall corporate structure. A media center should be positioned so that it provides effective and efficient production services to all aspects of the organization, not just a few. For example, if a video group operates under the aegis of a training department, or one aspect of training (e.g., sales), it is likely that video will be perceived only as a training tool. Similarly, if the video operation is situated in an employee communications department, the likelihood is that video is perceived primarily as an employee communications tool. Yet video should not be thought of as only a training tool, or only an employee communications tool; it is both. In addition, it is a tool for management communications, sales promotion, and can be used for many other functions such as recruiting, security analysts relations, community relations, etc.

Therefore, it makes sense for the media center to be positioned in the organizational structure in such a way that it will not only be perceived as an organization-wide resource, but will also be accessible to everyone in the organization. While a media center should have an organizational relationship to other communications "content" functions e.g. public relations, marketing and training, it should not be supervised by one of these. The media center should be supervised by an organizational staff group, such as a "General Services" department, not one tied to communications content.

HELPING THE ORGANIZATION SOLVE
COMMUNICATION PROBLEMS

A media center positioned in a non-communications content staff group should help the organization solve its communications problems. Figure 3.4 presents a schematic of the process of communications problem-solving in a hypothetical organization. First, the problem is expressed by an internal (employee) or external public (1). The organization, or department, (2) perceives that a communications problem exists. The organization, or department (3), then seeks resources to solve the problem. It confers with (4) several communications activities in order to get the job done: the graphic arts department, training, video operations, AV services,

Figure 3.4: Organizational Communications
Problem-Solving Model

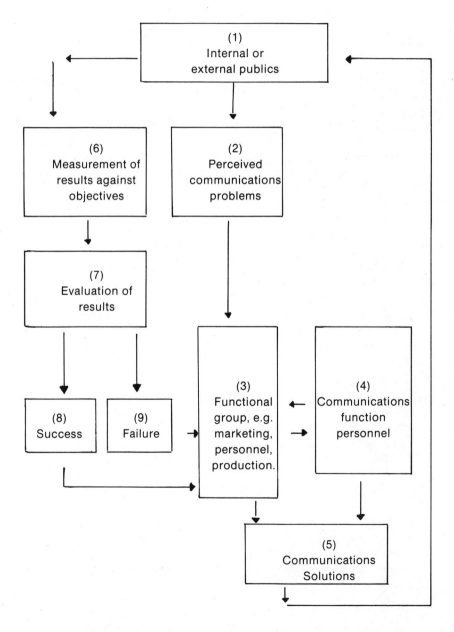

public relations, and so on. The communications solution (media) (5) whether a teleconference, video disc, multimedia production, video tape program, audio tape program, film, slide program, photograph, graphic or print piece, is then delivered to the internal or external public (1). These publics react to the solution and the results are measured against communications objectives (6). These results are evaluated (7) as either successful (8) or unsuccessful (9). At this point the results are fed back to the functional group (3), which will have to decide on the need for future action. The primary role of the media center in this system is to help translate the perceived problem into a media solution that will bring about the desired results.

THE PRESSING NEED TO COORDINATE

When media production activities are spread out all over the organizational map, it will take longer than might otherwise be necessary to bring together all the required resources to solve a problem. Moreover, with many different departments getting into the act, the job of coordinating problem-solving efforts is much more difficult. If the media production functions are scattered among various organizational departments, it follows that the production personnel are also scattered. However, if all media production functions and personnel are consolidated into one department serving the entire organization, the personnel and equipment can and should serve as an effective resource for the entire organization.

This consolidation allows all communications media personnel (writers, graphic artists, producer/directors and photographers) to meet under one roof to provide a professional level of media production services. It also becomes easier to determine production priorities and provide media consulting and production services to the organization in an organized manner. When media production functions are separated, one department may unwittingly place the production of a low priority program ahead of other more important programs, to everyone's detriment.

Bringing together all the communications personnel, media and hardware into one unit helps to increase the level of professionalism. Experience suggests that all too often content experts attempt to produce communications programs without the skills of a professional communicator. By creating a centralized media operation, the potential exists for separating those who create content (marketing, sales, finance, personnel, research and development, planning) from those who can translate it into a language and form that can be understood by various publics. A corollary advantage is that communications personnel will usually have a more objective perspective on the content.

Perhaps it may not have been appropriate to suggest the centralization outlined above 25 years ago, but it is warranted today, and even more so as a concept for the future. Our culture is becoming increasingly entangled in a network of communications. At the heart of the matter is communications technology. The increased number of communications networks that speed information from point to point and the increased access and usage of communications technology affects all organizational employees. (This topic is explored more fully in Chapter 10, The Evolving Media Center.)

More than ever, organizations are faced with the pressing need to make decisions regarding not only what will be communicated to internal and external publics, but how this information will be communicated. The "what" is a top level policy decision; the "how" is an operational decision made by the combination of various organizational departments, communications functions and the media production group. Organizations plan years ahead with respect to marketing objectives, staffing requirements, capital needs, future cashflow and future facilities. It is time to plan for the future internal and external communications needs of the organization by centralizing media operations and making them accessible to the entire organization.

FOOTNOTES

1. Eugene Marlow, *Communications and the Corporation* (New York: United Business Publications, Inc., 1978).

4

Staffing the Media Center

One of the hardest decisions a corporate media center manager faces is when and how to expand personnel. This chapter offers some guidelines for staffing the media center with respect to what types of positions need to be filled; the qualifications necessary to each; where to find the appropriate personnel; and how to keep them.

IDENTIFYING THE POSITIONS TO BE FILLED

The number and type of positions needed in the corporate media center will vary depending on the level of the organization's media production activites. On the simplest level, take an organization in which very little production originates in-house; outside agencies handle most of the work. In this case, the organization should at least designate someone to serve as the media production liaison, or ombudsman. Ideally, this person would be situated in a communications activity. In organizations where several individuals purchase media services from outside agencies, these people should have some experience, and perhaps training, in media production so they can accurately judge the quality of their purchases. Moreover, the organization's central purchasing department must be aware of these activities and monitor the propriety of contractual obligations.

As corporate media production activities increase, so will the need for media professionals. Eventually, the organization may need to consider hiring individuals with expertise in the three major media areas (graphic arts, film and electronic), each of which will be discussed in turn.

See me
John D.

APPLICATION
FOR
EMPLOYMENT

FOR OFFICE USE ONLY	
Work Location _D4_	Rate
Position	Date

PERSONAL

Date __May 14__

Name __Srith__ __Sam__ __S.__
      Last   First   Middle

Social Security No. __061-44-43.5__

Present address __4 Main St.__ __New York__ __New York__ __10022__
    No.   Street   City   State   Zip   Telephone No. __212-225-1257__

Are you legally eligible for employment in the U.S.A.? __✓__

State age if under 18 or over 70

What method of transportation will you use to get to work? __bus__

Position(s) applied for __video engineer__   Rate of pay expected _____ per week

Would you work Full-Time __✓__ Part-Time _____ Specify days and hours if part-time _____

Were you previously employed by us? __no__ If yes, when? _____

Are there any other experiences, skills, or qualifications which you feel would especially fit you for work with our organization? _____

__See Resume__

RECORD OF EDUCATION

School	Name and Address of School	Course of Study	Check Last Year Completed				Did You Graduate?	List Diploma or Degree
Elementary			5	6	7	8	☐ Yes ☐ No	
High	_See Resume_		1	2	3	4	☐ Yes ☐ No	
College			1	2	3	4	☐ Yes ☐ No	
Other (Specify)			1	2	3	4	☐ Yes ☐ No	

(Turn to Next Page)

Graphic Arts

The graphic arts area should be staffed with a professional artist who is adept at both conceptualization and execution. If the volume of graphic arts work is high enough, the organization could consider hiring two individuals; one graphic artist (an art director or graphics designer), and one mechanical artist.

Film Production

Film production could be approached similarly: at the very minimum, a professional photographer should be hired who is skilled in the various film formats starting with still photography (black and white, color and 35mm transparency). Motion photography (cinematography) can be handled by the photographer or freelancers. The organization might be lucky enough to find an individual with expertise in both still and motion photography. However, while there are certainly common characteristics between the two, there are also many differences, and stretching one individual to handle both kinds of photography could turn out to be penny-wise and pound foolish. If the production volume in the film unit calls for dividing the film production group into two areas, it can be divided between a still photographer and a photo lab technician on the one hand, and a cinematographer on the other.

Electronic Media Production

A similar division of labor can be made in electronic media production. The advertisements of hardware manufacturers to the contrary, electronic hardware (such as television cameras and video tape recorders) of even the simplest design cannot be operated or maintained by just anyone. If an organization has enough work to warrant the purchase of video production and post-production equipment, it should staff the electronic media production section with not only one qualified producer/director, but a video engineer or technician as well.

The software (producer/director) and hardware (engineering) functions should be separated in the electronic media section. One reason is that the higher the level of complexity on the technological scale, the higher the degree of specialization required. While electronic media production equipment (cameras, for example) and post-production editing equipment have become more accessible to so-called non-professionals, their set-up and maintenance remains a problem. For example, there are television cameras on the market today that, with the proper sequence of switch flipping, will go through various set-up steps and be ready for use. However, if the camera breaks down in any way, a professional engineer and/or technician needs to be on hand to fix the problem. The same is true of computer-type electronic editing systems.

Further Staffing Considerations

There is another consideration with respect to staffing. Many organizations stretch their in-house media staffs by having personnel double up on tasks: graphic artists perform film production tasks, film production personnel are asked to get involved with electronic media production, etc. In other organizations, personnel in communications activities such as employee relations or corporate communications are asked to perform media production functions part-time. Experience has shown that media production activities require attention on a full-time basis, if the final product is to be professional. Moreover, while there are similarities among the three production groups, there are many specific skills requisite to each area; imaging for print, for example, is quite different from presenting a visual image in film or in electronic media. Furthermore, the mechanics for producing a media product for print, film or video are quite different. Finally, it is the rare individual who can go from being a still photographer in the morning to a video producer/director in the afternoon, and still turn out a professional product.

Importance of Specialization

As the media center's workload increases, and as additional personnel are hired, the more specialized each function should become. For example, in a very active graphic arts group, the organization may be required to have several graphic designers and mechanical artists on staff. The graphic arts group may designate specific personnel to handle particular applications, such as promotional literature or communications. Others may be specifically assigned to design graphics for slides.

The film production group may similarly tend to specialize, with some individuals assigned to studio photography, and others to field photography. Still others can be designated to handle lab work such as film development and duplication. The slide production group may follow a similar pattern, with divisions between personnel using slide production origination equipment (such as Oxberry or Forox) and those developing and mounting the slides. Depending on the organization, this section might also require one person who handles the client/production interface —perhaps the manager in charge of slide production, or an assistant manager.

As the electronic media production group widens its scope of activity, it too may need more specialized personnel. For instance, in addition to a producer/director and a video engineer, this unit may eventually require video technicians, audio engineers and technicians, production assistants and so on.

The administrative section could expand to include AV specialists to handle media presentations, librarians to develop and manage a media library and one or more administrative assistants to handle the flow of paperwork associated with invoices, billing, and scheduling media production activity.

Thus the number of potential positions in a media production function ranges from one to several dozen, depending on the level and complexity of the media center's production activity.

QUALIFICATIONS OF MEDIA CENTER PERSONNEL

The Media Center Manager

What is a media center manager? What role does he or she take on that are substantively different from those of graphics artists, mechanical artists, photographers, producer/directors and the various technicians associated with the media center? Moreover, what are the characteristics of an effective media center manager?

To begin with, media managers share characteristics with their counterparts in other areas. In the *Effective Executive,* Peter Drucker offers five characteristics of an effective executive:

(1) Effective executives know where their time goes. They work systematically at manging the little of their time that can be brought under control.

(2) Effective executives focus on outward contribution, and gear their efforts to results rather than work. They start out with the question "What results are expected of me?" rather than with the work to be done, let alone with its techiques and tools.

(3) Effective executives build on strengths — their own strengths; the strengths of their superiors and subordinates; and on the strengths of the situation, that is, on what they can do. They do not build on weakness. They do not start out with things they cannot do.

(4) Effective executives concentrate on the few major areas where superior performance will produce outstanding results. They force themselves to set priorities and start with their priority decisions.

(5) Effective executives, finally, make effective decisions. They know that this is, above all, a matter of system — of the right steps in the right sequence.[1]

To these characteristics we can add several others that distinguish an effective and successful media center manager.[2]

Entrepreneurial spirit

An entrepreneur is someone who organizes and manages any enterprise, especially in business, usually with considerable initiative and risk. Other definitions state that the entrepreneur is the one who puts capital, labor and resources together in an enterprise that did not exist before and makes a business out of it.

The element of initiative and risk is a recurrent theme. Of course, not everyone is expected to go out and, at considerable financial risk, pull capital, labor and resources together to start a business. But there is much to be said for the spirit of this kind of activity. Being a manager in an existing organization does not mean that risk and initiative are eliminated. On the contrary, in an age of information, where change is the norm, today's manager must have the ability to take risks and some initiative; it is this "spirit" that separates the merely adequate from the outstanding manager. Moreover, this kind of spirit is not just reserved for the highest echelons of the organization, but is requisite to all levels of the organizational structure. Without it, no new product will surface, no department will flourish and no employee will advance very far.

Marketing skills

A media manager must have the ability to market and promote his area. The manager must be able to convince others and keep them convinced, that his area has worth and should be supported. This means developing a network of clients (supporters in the organization/political sense), garnering recognition for employees and what they do and getting people to come back for more. (See Chapter 6, Day to Day Operations.)

Administrative skills

All media managers must have administrative skills. What is crucial is to have an understanding of the administrative system within the department and the larger organizational system. Each department in an organization has an adminstrative system: an organizational chart; an expense budget;

accounts to be kept; forms, files and figures to be organized; performance reviews; budget reviews; quality control checks; planning procedures. Moreover, no department exists in a vacuum; each relates to the larger organizational network. This means the media center manager must be cognizant of organization-wide personnel policies (employee benefits, salary ranges, performance rating systems, etc.) in addition to keeping up with management changes and determining the effect of these changes on the department.

Human relations skills

The successful media manager must relate well to people. Machines, administrative systems and formal policies alone do not run organizations; people do. The manager who doesn't understand people at an elementary level is doomed to failure. The successful manager will have a deep understanding of people, knowing, for example, that what people say and what they do can be entirely different, and that the causes of people's actions are not necessarily direct.

Technical skills

Although there are exceptions, most people enter the management ranks from positions where they had mastered a particular skill: accounting, marketing, engineering, communications, media production, etc. It never hurts for the manager to have some technical skills in the area he or she is managing. While there are those that say a good manager can manage anything, a good manager can also fail without an adequate understanding of the technical skills applied to the particular area. If the manager doesn't have at least a basic understanding of the required technical skills (here, in media production) it must be acquired.

Communication skills

A successful media manager must be able to communicate formally and informally, in writing and verbally. Well-honed writing skills are a must, whether for preparing a short memo or an annual departmental report. The ability to communicate effectively and efficiently in writing and orally can help overcome deficiencies in other areas.

Flexibility

The competent media center manager must be flexible. Change is constant and adaptive abilities are what keep the species viable. If the media manager understands change and has developed mechanisms for dealing with it, and the stress that normally accompanies it, then this manager can help others adapt to change.

Production Personnel

Production personnel can be divided into three groups: software personnel, hardware personnel and administrative personnel. Software personnel would include: art directors, graphic artists, still photographers, cinematographers, slide designers, producers, directors, writers and media production assistants. Hardware personnel include: mechanical artists, photolab technicians, audio engineers, video engineers and audiovisual specialists and technicians. Administrative personnel include: administrative assistants, clerks and librarians.

As mentioned previously, there are essential differences between software and hardware personnel. In this context, software personnel usually have direct contact with media center clients. Art directors, still photographers and producer/directors have the primary task of helping to translate a client's ostensible comunications needs (see Chapter 5, Solving Communications Problems) into a communications form. Software personnel have the responsibility of shepherding a media project from initiation, to completion, to evaluation. The role and responsibility of hardware personnel, on the other hand, is to support the activities of software personnel by using and maintaining the tools and equipment necessary to execute the communications project, whether graphic (print), photographic or electronic.

Examining the Candidate's Background

There are four areas to consider in choosing the appropriate individual for a position in the organizational media center operation:

- Experience
- Education
- Knowledge and skills
- Interpersonal skills

Experience

Experience affords the greatest test of how appropriate a person is for a media production position, whether it is managerial, software, hardware or administrative. An individual with five or ten years of experience as a still photographer is obviously more skilled than one who has just graduated with a degree in communications arts. However, there are other factors with regard to experience that must be weighed. What is the quality of the individual's experience? Did the individual's skills grow during the last five to ten years? How effective or successful was the individual at the previous place of employment?

There may be times when an organization chooses to employ an individual with little experience. First, less experienced personnel will generally require less compensation. Second, older hires are not necessarily more experienced in what the organization *needs* than younger ones. To a degree, new communications technologies and the rapid rate of change weaken the argument for experience as a criteria for future performance. On the other hand, experience also brings with it maturity, understanding and judgment, which can be valuable assets in a candidate.

Education and training

Education is another criterion for selecting personnel. While it is not necessary that all members of the media staff have an undergraduate degree, it would be preferable, particularly for managerial and software personnel, primarily because these two groups will have contact with organizational executives, clients and subject experts. The credential of a college degree provides at least some educational parity between media center staff and the organizational clients. What kind of education is preferable? Management personnel are perhaps the most diffficult to define, particularly since there may not be a direct relationship between the college degree earned and potential success as a media center manager. Training in the software and hardware aspects of various media, as well as in verbal and written communications skills, is helpful. Formal education in business subjects is also useful, particularly in economics, accounting, marketing, sales, computer science, management information systems, personnel administration and organizational theory.

Software personnel should be trained in the various skills for which they are hired. For example, a graphic or mechanical artist should have some formal education in graphic arts, a photographer should have formal training in photography, etc. Producer/directors, on the other hand, should have formal hands-on training not only in television, a studio, film or multimedia, but also in written and verbal skills.

Hardware personnel, such as photo lab technicians, should have highly specific formal training in their areas. Video and audio engineers should have formal education in electronics, whether from a high school, college, university, military or trade institution.

Of course, there will be exceptions where individuals demonstrate knowledge of management, software production and hardware without the benefit of a formal education. In general, an individual's formal educational background should be weighed against his or her level of experience and demonstrated skills.

A person's knowledge, skill and abilities, particularly in software and hardware, should be demonstrable: a graphic or mechanical artist should be able to demonstrate these skills; a photographer should be able to display a portfolio of previous work and discuss which camera, what kind of lighting and what type of developing process were used; a producer/director should be able to present a "show reel" of previously produced video, film or multimedia programs, and discuss the various software and technical problems associated with each. Naturally, it will help if the candidate is interviewed by someone who has some knowledge of media production, which is why it is important that an organization have at least one person on board with such knowledge.

Interpersonal skills

Interpersonal skills are essential for any position on the media center staff. Even though managerial and software personnel (and to a degree administrative support personnel) will have more contact with organizational executives, clients and subject experts than will hardware personnel, there is no reason for anyone on the media center staff to have poor interpersonal communications skills. To a very large degree, an effective media center depends on the level of its people's interpersonal skills (please also see Chapter 7). While there is no substitute for software and technical skill, the ability to understand client problems at all levels in the organization, and the ability to work with others are qualities that help the media center make an effective and efficient contribution to the organization.

Desirable interpersonal skills and qualities might include the following abilities:

getting along with others
relating to management and creative personnel
dealing with subordinates and superiors
common sense, analytical and logical thinking
attention to detail while seeing the larger system
forming cogent arguments
organization
working well under pressure
enthusiasm and motivation
a positive attitude and willingness to work

strong verbal skills	being a self-starter
listening	being dynamic, yet mature
curiosity and creativity	a sense of showmanship, where
aggressiveness	appropriate
patience	a quick study

This emphasis on interpersonal skills and personal qualities may seem overdone. However, the functional objective of the media center is to provide the organization with effective and efficiently produced communications products. Therefore, media center staff should reflect a high degree of communication skills when dealing with executives, clients, subject experts or outside resources.

WHERE TO FIND STAFF

Promoting from Within

There are various sources for finding potential media center staff. The first and most obvious is the internal staff of the organization. Graphic artists could be found from the mechanical artists' ranks; photographers could come out of the photo lab; producer/directors could be promoted from the ranks of technical or production assistants.

External Resources

Another source is other organizations. As a result of the growth of media centers, increasing numbers of organizations can provide a pool of candidates who are already experienced in media management, software or hardware related activities.

Executive recruiters (commonly referred to as head-hunters) and employment agencies can also be a source of potential candidates. On the positive side, head-hunters may have more immediate access to appropriate candidates. On the other hand, they will charge a fee for their services, usually a percentage of the annual salary agreed upon between the hiring organization and the candidate.

Professional organizations may also provide leads (see Appendix II for a list of professional organizations).Some professional organizations maintain a job-matching service for members. Sometimes, those with newsletters regularly or periodically publish lists of available members for employment. Organizations looking for potential candidates can often publicize themselves in these newsletters.

Advertising in professional or trade journals is another route. Most communications and media production professionals read at least one professional or trade journal. The candidate the organization is looking for might be found by advertising in these publications (a listing of professional and trade journals is found in Appendix III).

Educational institutions, such as high schools, colleges or universities with specific communications programs (either software or technical), or trade schools can also be an invaluable source for potential staff. Very often these institutions provide students with an employment service to match potential employers with graduating students and alumni. In addition, some institutions seek to have their students employed as interns. (Appendix IV lists a digest of colleges and universities with communications programs.)

Organizations can also find candidates by advertising in widely read publications, such as *The Wall Street Journal, The New York Times* or regional and local publications.

MANAGING THE STAFF

In addition to staffing the media center with qualified people, the successful media manager must also consider some of the aspects of managing creative media production personnel. First, it helps to think of creativity in terms of three main elements: an ability to make order out of chaos; an ability to put two unlike things together which result in a third thing; and knowing how to take this new thing formed out of chaos and communicate it in its simplest terms in such a way that it is both informative and entertaining. The major difference between the designations of creative and non-creative personnel is that the former involves more highly developed skills based on inherent abilities. It is really a matter of degree, not kind.

The first step toward practical, yet creative, management of the media center staff is to make order out of chaos. Job descriptions are essential. They give the manager and staff a starting point for understanding performance. A second step is the creation of performance standards. While a job description is a word picture of what the job is, a performance standard is a word description of what the individual will accomplish over a certain time period. Both documents serve as a dynamic, evolving foundation for the work to be performed.

A third and important aspect of managing the creative staff is to provide adequate compensation. Creativity might provide psychological compensation for a while, but sooner or later the good staff will need monetary compensation as well. Creative personnel also enjoy the feeling that there is a chance for upward mobility. If a career ladder doesn't exist, create one.

That young AV technician pushing around slide projectors may one day become a senior production supervisor.

Apart from these formalities, the most important service a media center manager can provide for the staff is an environment for the development of creativity. This means that the manager must have a feel for the creative process. Moreover, the manager must know when to challenge fiercely and when to lay off. Each creative person is different and even creative geniuses have dry spells.

Exchange of information is a natural part of the creative environment. Staff meetings are an ideal way for creativity to be stimulated, honed and channeled. Providing the opportunity for staff to attend professional conferences and seminars is another way. All these kinds of information gathering activities help the creative person to expand his or her horizons, to grow, develop and make an even larger contribution to the unit. The manager needs to encourage the creative staff to continue to seek new information, as well as to develop interesting and effective new ways to communicate it.

FOOTNOTES

1. Peter F. Drucker, *The Effective Executive* (New York: Harper & Row, 1967), pp. 23-24.

2. Some portions of this chapter are adapted, with permission, from Eugene Marlow, "To Manage or Not to Manage," *Videography*, February 1980, Copyright United Business Publications, Inc.

5

Solving Communications Problems

For a corporate media center to be successful it must have an operating approach that makes it a contributor to the overall and long-term development of the organization. To be effective, the media center staff should adopt a systems perspective of the organization. It is imperative that, regardless of the function or position, media center personnel understand that they are not working in a vacuum, but are performing a service within the context of the larger corporate training, employee communications and external communications systems.

Successful communication is not easy. As I pointed out in a previous publication,[1] there are at least nine reasons why communications, no matter what the medium, fail:

(1) Failure to define the communications problem.
(2) Failure to define the objectives of the communication.
(3) Failure to measure the results of the communication against the objectives.
(4) Failure to profile the intended audience.
(5) Failure to take into account where the intended audience is and in what environment it will receive the communication.
(6) Failure to determine whether the communication will prove cost-effective.
(7) Failure to ascertain which medium (or media) will be the most communications-effective.

(8) Failure to define how the program will be produced (pre-production planning; production; post production; duplication; and distribution).

(9) And, most importantly, failure to evaluate whether the communication succeeded or failed, and why.

Turning these negative statements into positive questions, we can develop an approach to communications problem-solving by asking:

(1) Is there a communications problem?

(2) What are the objectives of the communication?

(3) How will the results of the communication be measured against the objectives?

(4) What is the profile of the intended audience?

(5) Where is the intended audience and in what environment will it receive the communication?

(6) Will a formal communication prove cost-effective.

(7) What medium (or media) will be the most communications-effective?

(8) How will the program be produced?

(9) Did the communication succeed or fail, and why?

IS THERE A COMMUNICATIONS PROBLEM?

In most instances, clients come to the media center with problems that are truly communications-related. In certain cases, however, the communications needs may be more apparent than real; i.e. media may not be the answer to the problem. Blindly producing communications programs for apparent communications needs only serves to perpetuate the myth that communications in any form can and will solve any problem, and that the mere act of producing and communicating a program will automatically do the job.

Therefore, it is important to know whether the client has indeed come to the right place. In some cases, the answer will be easily determined, either because the communications problem is simple or because the client has adequately determined and defined the problem and objectives. However, if a client is unable to articulate the problem or define objectives, he or she may be seeking a solution to what is not a communications problem. For example, a West Coast company was experiencing a decrease in morale on the part of the sales force, and sales were declining markedly. The company decided that the sales force needed more training and/or some sort of motivation, and called in a consultant to prepare a program. After a period of research, the consultant discovered that the problem was really administrative: the salesmen were not receiving their commission checks within a reasonable period of time following the close of a sale. The consultant recommended ways to streamline the system for issuing commission checks. Once the check delivery system was speeded up, morale and sales increased.

DEFINING THE OBJECTIVES OF THE COMMUNICATION

Objectives should be clearly spelled out in specific terms for all to understand. To be effective, the program's objective must be defined in such concrete language and terms that it will provide a criterion for the measure of success (or failure) of the communication. In other words, objectives should also serve as a yardstick: how much money did the program help generate, how much was efficiency increased, how much was productivity enhanced, how much money was saved, etc.

Robert F. Mager suggests an excellent method for defining training and instructional objectives.[2] (While his programmed learning text is designed primarily for teachers, it can also be used effectively by media professionals.) In summary, Mager provides the following structure:

(1) A statement of instructional objectives is a collection of words describing one of your intents.

(2) An objective will communicate your intent to the degree you have described what the learner will be doing when demonstrating achievement and how you will know when he is doing it.

(3) To describe terminal behavior (what the learner will be doing):
a. identify and name the overall behavior act.
b. define the important conditions under which the behavior is to occur.
c. define the criterion of acceptable performance.

(4) Write a separate statement for each objective: the more statements you have, the better the chance you have of making clear your intent.

MEASURING RESULTS

Measuring the success or failure of communication programs (and hence, the clarity and reliability of the statement of objectives) is easier for some programs than for others. Communications content can be defined on two levels: (1) content that makes knowledge more productive —

communications that motivate individuals to learn new skills, the results of which can be translated directly into more efficient corporate operations, sales and earnings; and (2) content that creates understanding — communications programs that bring vital information to employees so they have a better understanding of the context in which they are working. The results of communications in the former group are easier to measure and analyze than those in the latter group. However, the effectiveness of both kind of communications programs must be measured in some form.

To develop yardsticks to measure change against objectives it is necessary to first assess the current situation. Assume, for example, that a training program is expected to increase production in a manufacturing plant by 10%. In order to do so one must determine the current level of productivity. In other words, to effectively measure any changes resulting from the new training program, the post-testing results must have a base, or control, from which to draw comparisons. Once this base has been established one can determine whether the new communications training program has succeeded.

Several kinds of changes can be measured, such as a change in quantity, or a change in attitude. A change in quantity is simply a measure of numbers. For example, analysis may show that x number of people produce 20 widgets per hour. After dissemination of the communications program (say an interactive video disc or video tape program), evaluation may show that productivity is now 30 widgets per hour, an increase of 50%.

When evaluating for a change in attitude, one can use a variety of scales, including a Likert Scale (a five-point scale in which the interval between each point on the scale is equal) or a semantic-differential scale (usually a seven point scale).[3] The Likert scale provides responses ranging from "strongly agree" to "strongly disagree;" a semantic differential scale provides a respondent with bi-polar responses (such as "original" as opposed to "conventional"). For example, prior to a communications program, a salesman may be negatively disposed to an impending sales territory reorganization as measured on a Likert scale. Following the dissemination of a communications program (e.g. video tape and/or print) outlining the advantages of the reorganization, a Likert scale would be a useful instrument for measuring any change in attitude.

Change can most easily be gauged, comparatively speaking, for skills training programs, primarily because such programs involve specific steps in a process to be learned. For example: "After the training sessions, the mechanics will be able to turn five widgets in 10 seconds, with a 95% degree of accuracy." Motivation programs are the hardest to measure because the degree of change in motivation may or may not be immediately obvious; the audience may need time to digest and respond to the motivational aspect of the communication.

PROFILING THE INTENDED AUDIENCE

Knowing the market is an inherent part of the marketing process. Rather than products and services, however, media producers market and sell information that (1) makes knowlege more productive, and (2) creates understanding. No organization should attempt to produce communications without first knowing some of the basic facts about the intended audience such as:

- Male, female, or both?
- Age groupings?
- Management, professional, staff, clerical, external?
- Level of work experience?
- How many?

Another aspect to the audience profile question has to do with the nature of the audience's perceptions. One simple technique for determining the audience's perceptions is to seek out a portion of the prospective audience and listen! Almost any worthwhile handbook on business communications recommends this procedure. This technique shows that what the information source (e.g., management) believes are the communications needs and what the receiver (e.g., customers, employees) believes these needs to be, are sometimes two very different things. Questioning part of the prospective audience can help obviate the trap of communicating information in a manner inappropriate to the audience's needs.

One net result of this process is that the audience will tell the communicator how the so-called communication should be prepared. The whole process should result in a more effective communication; i.e. the chances of achieving the defined objectives will be enhanced. Moreover, finding out the facts about the audience (the demographic perceptions) will have a direct effect on the style and language of the communication.

LOCATION OF THE AUDIENCE

The location of the intended audience could have a direct influence on the choice of media. To determine this, certain questions must be considered:

Will an audience congregate in a central location or several locations to receive the program?
Does the program have to be portable?
Are there competent individuals available to present the program?

Must the program be available to anyone at any time?

Is there a need to distribute the program in various media?

Will large groups or small groups receive the communication, or both?

What is the life of the program in relationship to the audience? Will it be received once; several times in a short period of time; in several locations at the same time; or will the program be used for several years; or go to several different types of audiences?

Is the audience in the United States or in various overseas locations?

Questions such as these must be analyzed before choosing the production technique and distribution medium because it may turn out that the production medium and distribution will have to be different. Assume, for example, that the communications program involves sales promotion and that the salesperson must bring the program into a prospective client's office. Obviously, the media choices will have to match the varying environments. The salesperson would have some difficutly lugging a ¾-inch video cassette unit and monitor from office to office, whereas a portable super 8mm unit would do the job admirably.

Knowing where the audience is will affect how many units of distribution hardware will be needed. For example, it may be that a sales force is scattered in a relatively small geographic area and it is important that a subject expert be present following the formal communication. In this case, it could be decided that the formal communication can be hand carried by the subject expert from location to location over an extended period of time. On the other hand, if analysis shows that formal communications programs will be distributed to the sales force over a period of time, then a more permanent distribution network may be decided on, e.g. a video cassette or video disc network.

COST-EFFECTIVENESS OF FORMAL COMMUNICATION

Cost-effectiveness refers to how desirable it is to spend x amount of dollars for y amount of results. Of extreme importance in the communications problem-solving process, cost-effectiveness is the factor that management and individual clients look at when determining the desirability of producing a formal communications program, or when deciding whether to initiate a broad communications function (e.g. a video cassette network). The dollar figure will also help determine whether one communications medium should be chosen over another.

In this discussion, the term "formal communications" refers to information conveyed in a structured and succinct manner, and does not apply to interpersonal communications in which no formal media presentations are involved. Greeting the secretary in the morning is an informal communication; a 10-minute film on the company's dental plan is a formal communication.

An objective way of approaching the cost-benefit/medium choice is to determine what will be gained by creating a formal communication. There are various angles from which cost-effectiveness can be viewed:

(1) What is the cost per person of one medium vs. another?
(2) What will it cost if content is not formalized?
(3) Will the formal communcation help increase revenue?
(4) Will the formal communication help reduce expenses?

Cost-Per-Person Comparisons

For example, one can determine how many people will actually receive the communication over a period of time. If, for instance, a $5000 video program dealing with training skills will be viewed by 10,000 employees over a period of one year, the cost-per-viewer is 50 cents, plus employee viewing time. However, a cost-per-person analysis is, at best, only a tool to weigh the financial advantages of distribution by one medium as opposed to another. It may be cheaper to distribute the information via print (e.g., a booklet), and it may turn out that, everything else being equal, the "cost-per" via print is less than 50 cents. Of course, distribution costs are not the only consideration; if they were, then the cheapest route to follow would be word of mouth (extemporaneous communication) rather than any formal communication. Word of mouth, of course, allows for no control or uniform delivery of information, and could take forever. However, an analysis of distribution costs on a "cost-per" basis can be a useful starting point.

Reducing Individual Time Investment

Cost-effectiveness can be viewed from other angles. For example, can a communications program reduce the amount of time currently needed to learn skills in an existing training situation? Assuming that conventional training methods (stand-up lecture, on-the-job training, programmed instruction booklets, operating manuals) require ten hours of a student's time, will a new communications program reduce the amount of time invested (with the same degree of results or better) than an existing program? If the answer is yes, then cost-effectiveness is at work. Again, the cost of the new communications program must be compared to the cost-effective advantages gained by using it.

Increasing Revenues

Another aspect to the cost-effectiveness of communications programs, is that of profit. Many companies have discovered that communication media can be used effectively for external sales promotion — for instance, when a company wishes to make a sale to the president, chief operating officer, purchasing officer or high level vice president of another company. Many companies are using portable super 8mm film projectors (with rear and front screen capability) to make their pitch. Substantial profit can result from an investment in such programs. For example, a sales promotion program costing $30,000 can generate accounts of well over that amount, especially if the market involves the sale of a single product with a minimum cost of $30,000.

Making Better Use of the Time Available

Information derived from a subject expert that runs two hours in extemporaneous form can be condensed into a 20-minute video tape. But does this mean that the company saves an hour and 40 minutes of everybody's time? It may. In addition, the two hours can be put to better use: for example, the 20-minute video tape can be followed by an hour and 40-minute discussion session with the subject expert. The value of a subject expert, is not necessarily his or her ability to present valuable information time and again, but his or her ability to answer specific questions. Therefore, when an audience has the opportunity to ask questions and develop a dialogue with a subject expert, the chances are higher that the audience will have a better grasp of the material presented than if no repartee develops. This illustrates that while creating a formal communication may indeed save time and money, its cost-effectiveness does not stop there.

CHOOSING THE MOST
COMMUNICATIONS-EFFECTIVE MEDIUM

In addition to frequency, audience size and location, the inherent content of the communications must be analyzed in order to choose the most effective medium:

(1) Does the communication intend to teach motor skills, or attitude/behavior changes?
(2) Is the person delivering the content as important as the content itself?
(3) Is the content of the communication primarily factual in nature?
(4) Is the inherent content of the communication conceptual in nature?

Show Me

Ronald W. Spangenberg, for instance, has shown that motion is best taught in a media presentation, especially if the information is not easily conveyed verbally or the student are unfamiliar with the task, e.g. operating a machine. [4] Spangenberg's work suggests that a film, video tape or video disc presentation would be more desirable for teaching motor skills than a series of static slides.

These studies also suggest that where imitation is required —for example, learning an attitude via real life demonstration or role models —film, video or video disc are ideal media for communications effectiveness.

VIPs

Sometimes the person delivering the message is as important as the information itself. For example, executives are inherently important organizational figureheads. What they say is important because *they* are saying it. In this instance, a still slide or photograph together with an audio cassette recording will have less impact than if the audience sees the executives themselves. While a video or film communication is second best to having a live presentation, in-person appearances are not always possible or cost-effective, especially if the organization is geographically dispersed. But video or film remain far superior to a print or other static piece.

Video remains one of the most effective ways of motivating personnel. However, since video is once removed from personal contact, the type of material presented must be chosen carefully. Too often management falls into the trap of presenting on video the kind of motivational pep talk that may work well person-to-person, but which seldom transfers well to the video medium.

Just the Facts

Motion is not always required, especially if the inherent content of the communication is factual in nature.

If the communications problem involves teaching factual information, a person may not need to be part of the communication and motion may not have to be part of the presentation. The learner may be required to digest information in a pre-determined sequential manner. That is, first perform step A, then step B, step C, and so on. Factual information may involve mere numbers, such as those in a stockholders' annual report. Print in its many varieties, and other static communications media (slides), can communicate this type of information quite well. Research into the relative communications effectiveness of various media has shown that there is relatively little difference among them in cognitive learning of factual information. Goodman's research on factual learning, for example, found no significant differences in the relative effectiveness of sound motion pictures versus sound film strips when teaching safety topics to sixth and seventh graders. The results of a 1958 Allen, Cooney and Weintraub study testing sixth graders again showed that no significant differences in learning were observable between a 17-minute color motion sound picture and a set of 66 color slides. Four other studies (by Zuckerman, Lumsdaine, Roshal and Miller, respectively) comparing sound filmograph versus sound motion pictures, gave similar results to those for the comparison between slides and motion picture film.[5]

Concepts

Conceptual information is a different matter. One of the earliest and most important uses of video, for example, was to explain a process, particulary a process involving a concept normally difficult to grasp. Films and video tapes containing graphics and/or simple animation can explicate complex ideas faster and more easily than the printed word. Hovland, Lumsdaine and Sheffield's 1949 study compared a 50-minute filmstrip to a 43-minute motion picture training film. While no significant differences in learning of facts was found, the film proved to be significantly more effective where familiarity with three dimensional relationships was important in the learning material.[6]

Two studies by Wells, Van Mondrans, Postlethwait and Butler showed that motion pictures were more effective than still pictures or slides in presenting concepts involving time and motion, and that sequential still photographs and slides (in that order) were more effective in presenting concepts involving space.[7]

PRODUCING THE PROGRAM

The production process for any medium involves four stages:

(1) Pre-production planning
(2) Production
(3) Post-production
(4) Duplication and distribution

The pre-production stage is where all planning takes place. With respect to teleconferencing this might mean planning the meeting agenda. For video disc, video tape, film and multimedia presentations this step involves developing content outlines, determining where shooting will take place, developing production budgets, selecting necessary per diem personnel, making travel arrangements, casting, etc.

Production involves creating the actual elements of the program: drawing mechanicals, in the case of graphic arts; shooting, in the case of film and electronic media. During production, raw material is created for later refinement.

Post-production is another term for organizing the raw material created during the production phase. Post-production involves creating layouts and mechanicals in the case of graphic arts; and editing in the case of photographic/cinemagraphic and electronic media.

The last stage is duplication and distribution, making copies of approved, final communications programs (whether in print, slide, photographic, film, video tape or vide disc formats) and getting those programs to the appropriate audience.

EVALUATION

Once the communications program has been produced and distributed, it must be determined whether all the analysis, time, money and labor spent on producing the program achieved the desired results. Thus it is important to specify yardsticks, such as stated objectives, early in the process.

Communications should be evaluated at various stages of the program's development. Such evaluations may suggest beneficial changes of length, style of presentation, medium of communication, use and distribution of the finished product.

The simplest, yet most informal feedback mechanism would be to ask the client whether he or she felt that the communication succeeded or failed. On a more scientific level, formal questionnaires could accompany the communication program or be distributed to the audience some time after the communication has been received. The questionnaire might involve the use of Likert semantic differential scales, open ended questions or yes/no type responses. Questionnaires might also ask how many people at a particular location received the communication, if there were any technical problems and related questions. Questionnaires are further discussed in Chapter 6.*

If success has been achieved, go on to the next project! But if the desired results were not achieved, one should re-evaluate the whole process from the beginning. Was the communications problem properly defined? Were the weaknesses in any of the decisions made during the development of the communications product?

---

*Again, a basic text such as Tuckman is recommended.

FOOTNOTES

1. This material is adapted, with permission, from Eugene Marlow, *Communications and the Corporation,* Copyright 1978, United Business Publications, Inc.

2. Mager, Robert F., *Preparing Instructional Objectives* (Belmont, CA: Pitman Learning, Inc., 1975).

3. The reader is advised to refer to a basic research text, e.g., *Conducting Educational Research,* by Bruce W.Tuckman, 2nd ed., Harcourt Brace Jovanovich, Inc., 1978, to learn about these and other measurement methodologies.

4. Spangenberg, Ronald W., "The Motion Variable in Procedural Learning," *AV Communications Review,* 21 (4) (Winter 1973).

5. See *Sound Slide and Filmograph Presentations: A Review of Research and Application to Production,* by William H. Allen, League for Innovation in Community College, 1974, for discussions of these and other studies.

6. Ibid.

7. Wells, Russel F., Adrian P. Mondrans, S.N. Postlethwait and David C. Butler, "Effectiveness of Three Visual Media and Two Study Formats in Teaching Concepts Involving Time, Space and Motion," *AV Communications Review,* Summer 1973.

6

Day to Day Operations

COORDINATION AND SCHEDULING

Regardless of the size and complexity of the media center, coordination and scheduling are requisite to effectiveness and efficiency. In order to avoid missed deadlines, scheduling conflicts and just plain chaos, each major unit of the media center (electronic media, film, graphic arts and administration) must have mechanisms for scheduling and coordination. One of the most useful of these is a scheduling board.

Scheduling Board

A scheduling board can be set up using horizontal and vertical axes. The horizontal axis can provide time segments; daily, weekly, monthly, or a combination. Depending on the volume of work to be handled, the time frame might consist of daily slots for the three months, and weekly slots for the succeeding three months. The vertical axis can list the names of the personnel involved in each project and the name of the project. Individuals in the unit could be given color-coded magnetic dots.

Colors can also be used to distinguish among the various phases in a project's development (i.e., pre-production, production, post-production, duplication and distribution). Different magnetic tabs could be used to indicate if personnel are working on-site or on-location. This board allows the unit manager to immediately see potential scheduling conflicts (such as when the board indicates one person is scheduled to be in two places at the

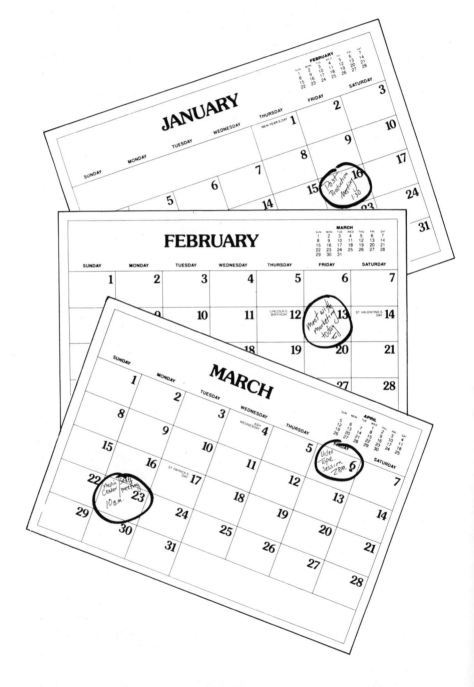

same time), when too much work is scheduled for one week and very little the next, if one individual is overloaded and others have a light work schedule, and so on. The board should be placed in an area where all personnel can view it.

Properly used, the scheduling board can reassure management that work is proceeding in an orderly and coordinated fashion. The board is also useful as a marketing tool for new clients who, when shown the board, realize that the unit is busy and productive.

Staff Meetings

Regular staff meetings, even if the group is small, are important for coordination. They provide opportunities for the manager to impart information, and for the staff to give the manager feedback on successes and failures, to raise questions and to provide recommendations. The staff meeting presents an opportunity for unit personnel to feel that they have a stake in the unit's success. Meetings also provide a forum for staffers to discuss current and future projects and the problems associated with them. The meetings can also serve as a time for personnel to review finished projects and receive feedback from the group on their perception of the project. These feedback sessions can be very valuable, especially if the manager wants to create an atmosphere of free exchange where personnel feel they can give and receive feedback without detriment to their egos or careers. This is much easier said than done. But the risk is worth taking, particularly if the manager wants to maintain a dynamic and open atmosphere where ideas are freely exchanged. Ultimately, everyone benefits.

Staff meetings can also be used for periodic broad looks at the progress of the media center, perhaps every six months. These meetings might start with a simple history of the operation, a "where did we come from?" scenario: When did the center begin? With what kinds of applications? What was the original staffing and budget? A good analysis can help dispel fuzzy perceptions about the center's progress.

Next, media center management might want to take stock of the client list. Who are the center's clients? Is there one client, several, a dozen? Who are its oldest clients? What about the most recent clients? What programs have been produced? Has there been a shift in emphasis? This analysis should uncover some trends and growth patterns.

Additional analysis might be made of the media center's staff. Are they competent? Partially trained? Ready for new challenges? And equipment—is it up-to-date or obsolete? What is the level of production costs— not just out-of-pocket expenses, but also the time spent on each project (on average) multiplied by hourly rates? How do production costs compare to post-production and duplication costs? Is there an imbalance? What are the average costs? How do these statistics compare to the average length per program? Is there a correlation?

FORMS, FORMS, FORMS

Paperwork is universal to every organizational media center. Basically, forms fall into four categories: (1) pre-production, (2) production, (3) post-production, and (4) general administrative. Effectively used, forms can serve a multitude of purposes and provide several benefits, such as the following:

- Serving as a guide to production personnel in the development of a project.
- Establishing a control system from which responsibilities can be delegated.
- Incorporating changes in a project.
- Providing reliable data for effective decision-making.
- Encouraging planning and control of production activities.
- Recording the history of each project and facilitating subsequent estimates of costs and schedules.

Pre-Production Forms

Pre-production forms allow virtually anyone in the media center to help a client determine what is required. Pre-production forms (also known as "requests for media production") should contain information such as is indicated in Figure 6.1.

Figure 6.1: Sample Request for Media Production Form

Date   Client   Job #
Subject   Project Title
Project Purpose (e.g., training, employee communications)
Medium (e.g., video tape film, audio tape)
Program Objectives
Program Content
Target Audience
Audience Size
Audience Location(s)
Distribution Format
Due Date   Estimated Budget
Approval Signatures   Production Schedule

Pre-production forms should also contain room for a complete production budget analysis. Table 6.1 lists the budget details required to completely cover all the items that could be involved in a multimedia, video disc, video or film program.

Table 6.1: Items to Include in a Production Budget

Crew

Producer
Director
Technical director
Lighting director
Camera operators
Video tape engineer
Audio engineer
Production assistant
Electricians
Grips
Make-up
Wardrobe
Scriptwrter
Set design
Casting

Travel Expenses

Auto rentals
Air fares
Hotels
Meals
Petty cash

Rental Expenses

Camera
Sound
Grip
Lighting
Generator
Dolly
Video tape recorders

Set Expenses

State rental
Carpenters
Grips
Electricians
Props
Hardware/paint/lumber
Special effects

Location Expenses

Location fees
Scouting camera
Guard/police

Graphics Expenses

Artwork
Supers
Slides
Stills

Stock Expenses

16mm film/develop
Video tape stock (½", ¾", 1", 2")
Audio tape stock

Talent Expenses

On-camera principals
On-camera extras
Voiceovers
Models

Table 6.1: Items to Include in a Production Budget (cont'd.)

Miscellaneous Expenses	Post Production Expenses
Administrative	Film (editors, opticals, animation,
Phone/Cables	special effects)
Messengers	Video tape (bump up protections,
Trucking	time coding, shooting artwork,
Petty cash	off-line editing, on-line editing,
	film-to-tape transfers, tape-to-film
	transfers)
	Stock footage
Distribution	Music
	Sound effects
Video disc	Narration/overdo studio
16mm film	Mixing studio
Super 8mm film	Transcriptions
¾" video cassettes	
½ reel-to-reel	
½ Betamax or VHS	
Slide dups	
Audio dups	
Shipping	

Budgetary forms for graphic arts and film production units might include items such as:

initial design and layout	pictorial
design revisions	original photography (loca-
typography	tion, studio, copy, portrait)
illustration	photography size (4x5, 8x10)
photography (black and	film color negative, color
white, color	transparency, black and)
photostats	white
word copy	number of originals (flat
tabular	art, double burns, kodaliths)
line graph	processing costs
bar chart	printing costs
pie chart	proofsheet costs
compound chart	duplication costs

The front part of the budget form should consolidate the aggregate costs of the four basic elements of the budget: pre-production, production, post-production and duplication and distribution. In this way, the client has a clear idea of the basic steps in the production process and how much each will cost. Moreover, each item on the budget form should have two columns: estimated costs and actual costs. As each phase of the production process is completed, the producer/director and the client will be able to track the efficiency of the production process *during* the course of production, rather than waiting until the program is "in the can," so to speak.

Other pre-production forms include: storyboards, location survey checklists, lighting plots, set designs, scheduling forms, engineering checklists and production personnel checklists. A storyboard is represented in Figure 6.2. An example of a scheduling form is shown in Figure 6.3.

Production Forms

Production forms consist of documentation taken during the actual making of the project. These include camera shot lists, scripts and release forms.

A script page contains the following information: writer, title of the program, video information and audio information (including on-camera audio, music, special effects and voiceover). Release forms (see Figure 6.4) protect an organization from liability when subjects are used in a photograph, slide presentation, film, video tape or multimedia presentation. The legal department can develop a release form.

Post-Production Forms

Post-production forms can include such documentation as editing worksheets and shot logs. Also in this category are customized labels for video discs, video cassettes, audio tapes, films and slide presentations, as well as video tape duplication requests, library request forms, mastertape labels, duplication labels and feedback forms.

Feedback forms help determine if a media project was a success or a failure, or if it achieved a measure of accomplishment somewhere between. The rationale for creating feedback mechanisms for media projects is for media production management to develop more control over the perceived success or failure of a particular project. Some organizations have developed elaborate feedback forms, while others rely simply on verbal (informal) feedback from clients. A feedback form for a video disc, video, film or slide program might consist of the following items:

Figure 6.2: Sample Storyboard

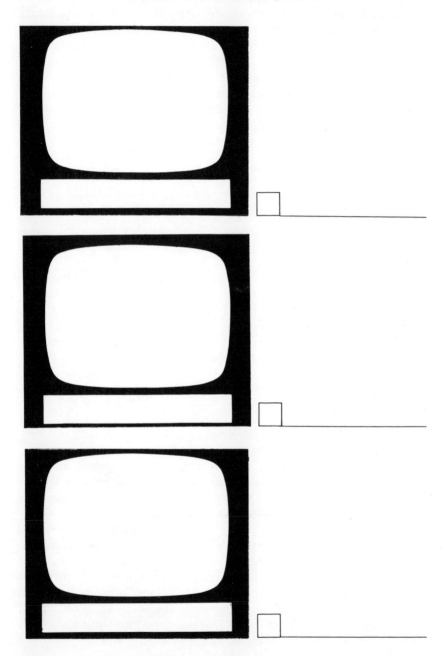

Figure 6.3: Graphic Arts Services Form

Job No.	Date In	Art Due	Project Due	Date Completed

☐ Design/General Artist/Designer

Special Instructions/Information

Total Hours

Project Phases	Sched. Time (Hrs.)	Date	Date	Scheduled Revision			Comments
				Due	Due	Due	
Initial Design & Layout							
Client Review							
Design Revision/Comprehensive							
Typography							
Illustration							
Photography							
Photostats							
Keyline/Assembly							
Approvals							
Production Specs.							
Totals							

Figure 6.4: Sample Authorization and Release Form

For value received, I give and grant to Company X, its affiliates, their successors and assigns and any person acting under its permission and authority (hereinafter called "company"), the unqualified right, privilege, and permission to reproduce in every manner or form, publish, and circulate video tapes, films, photographs, and transparencies of me and my property, and recordings of my voice, arising out of_____

and I hereby grant, assign, and transfer to Company X all my rights and interest therein.

I specifically authorize and empower Company X to cause any such video tapes, films, photographs, and transparencies of me and my property, and recordings of my voice, to be copyrighted or in any other manner to be legally registered in the name of Company X.

I, for myself, my heirs, executors, administrators and assigns, hereby remise, release, and discharge Company X for and from any and all claims of any kind whatsoever on account of the use of such video tapes, films, photographs, and transparencies of me and my property, and recordings of my voice, including but not limited to any and all claims for damages for libel, slander and invasion of the right of privacy.

I am of lawful age and of sound mind, and have read and understand this Authorization and Release.

Signed this_____of _____,
19____.

_____
Name

WITNESS:

_____   _____
                                Address

Title of program
Date
Size of audience
Kind of audience (internal, external, professional, hourly)
Technical problems (with the program or playback equipment)
Statement of objectives
A general question regarding the response compared to the program's objectives
A question regarding the technical quality of the program
An open-ended question, e.g. "further comments"
Respondent's location or organization

In addition, the name and address of the person to receive the feedback questionnaire should be prominent.

Administrative Forms

Forms which fall into this category include:

audiovisual equipment services
equipment trouble report
equipment repair/maintenance records
maintenance and inspection records
equipment operating logs
inventory logs (stock)
inventory logs (audiovisual equipment)
media library requests

Figures 6.5 and 6.6 give examples of two administrative forms.

INVOICES AND EXPENSE REPORTS

Since every organization will at some time use external resources to get a job done (e.g., scriptwriters, consultants, lighting designers, etc.) a system needs to be developed to handle the accompanying bills and paperwork. Regardless of the amount of work to be performed by an outside vendor, the corporate user should require the vendor to forward a formal statement of estimated charges and a statement of what he or she expects to do for the organization. This letter then becomes the estimate of charges. Similarly, the organization could send the vendor a statement of estimated charges along with a statement of the work it expects to be performed. This kind of documentation can then be forwarded to accounting. When bills

Figure 6.5: Maintenance or Inspection Record

DATE	SERVICE PERFORMED	TIME	PARTS USED	PRICE

Figure 6.6: Audiovisual Hardware Monthly Usage

_____
Month   Year

Hardware Type	Number of Requests	Average Loan Period	Total Hours	Comment

for the work begin to come in, the invoices can be checked against the statement of estimated charges. The statement of charges also provides the user with a check against estimates of time and additional charges.

Before the invoice is forwarded to accounting, however, the individual who contracted for the outside service should first check the invoice to make sure the service billed has been performed. This person should then initial and date the invoice, and forward it to the appropriate manager for further approval. In some organizations, systems have been developed whereby the client gives budget approval authorization to media production managers. This system authorizes the managers to approve invoices from outside vendors, as well as other bills, including internally generated charges, up to the limit of the approved budget. Therefore, once an invoice from an outside vendor has been approved, the manager can forward the invoice to accounting for payment, thereby avoiding the need for the client to see all the bills and become involved in a lot of paperwork.

There are some limits to this type of system, however, and these will depend on how each organization has set up its accounting checks and balances. In one organization, media production managers may have invoice approval authorization limits of $1000, while in another organization the limit might be $5000. Such limits may depend on what level the manager is in the organization. In any event, the unit manager or, at the very least, the media center manager, should negotiate the most flexible authorization limits, depending on the normal course of business. If 90% of all invoices for external services fall between $500 and $10,000, an authorization limit of $10,000 would seem sensible.

Before bills are forwarded to accounting or to the client for approval, copies should be filed in two places—in the project file and in a master invoice file. Depending on the volume of outside services, it might be wise to develop the master invoice file by vendor.

FILING SYSTEMS

Media production generates paperwork that reflects the history and cost of the project. A filing system therefore needs to be developed. Each organization will be different, of course, but no matter what form the filing system takes, it should at least provide easy access by management to any initiated, ongoing, or completed project. The system should also provide a basis for department management to develop cost analyses of the various aspects of the operation.

THE RATE CARD

As was mentioned in Chapter 2, after one or two years of practice, the media center should begin to develop a rate card for its services. By charging clients for media production services, the center can prove that it provides services at or near break-even; or, failing this kind of success, that media center production services should be modified in some way in order to make the center more cost-effective.

Rate cards should be developed for each major service offered in the media center. In "Administration," charges for the following services should be determined:

- conference room setups
- equipment loan out
- media distribution
- library loan out
- media presentations

The graphic arts unit could consider charges for these services:

- graphics design
- mechanicals

The film unit could charge for the following:

- slide design
- slide production
- still photography (studio)
- still photography (on-location)
- cinematography (director of photography)

The electronic media unit could charge for these services:

- pre-production (surveys/script supervision/travel time/engineering preparation)
- production
- post-production
- duplication (if in-house resources exist)

The charge-back items represent the labor expended by in-house personnel for media production work. The total cost of production will depend on the amount of labor expended, plus out-of-pocket expenses (scriptwriters, processing labs or printers, for example), in addition to so-called per diem expenses, such as ground and air travel, food and lodging, and other miscellaneous expenses.

The rate of labor charges for each activity outlined above will depend on many factors, the most important of which is what it would cost the clients to go outside for these services. If, for instance, clients can obtain a film at $3000 per finished minute outside, and it would cost the client $3500 a finished minute on average to produce the film in-house, the organization is better off using external resources (unless other forces such confidentiality or proprietorship preclude such activity). The rate of labor charges will also depend on the volume of work expected for the year. Given the volume of work and the amount of charge-back for labor, will this combination result in a profitable, break-even, or unprofitable media center operation at the end of the fiscal year?

The final consideration is what the will market bear. There is no reason why an organizational media center should not charge as much as it can for its services, while remaining cost-effective. For one thing, the higher the charges, the better the chances that a break-even operation will be realized. Secondly, higher charges seem to have a beneficial psychological impact on clients. Perhaps we can call this the Cadillac or Steinway syndrome: we expect to pay for quality. My own experience has been that low charges for media production services sometimes develop an attitude of low respect for the in-house operation.

High charges can also have an impact on the media center staff, giving them a sense of partaking in and contributing to a business. The service they provide brings money into the business. There is something psychologically invigorating in knowing that the service provided a client is going to make a difference to the survival of the unit.

COST ANALYSIS

A good filing system, good records and thoroughly filled out project forms can help facilitate the development of cost analysis. Each major unit of the media center should be able to provide the media center manager with at least quarterly, if not monthly, reports on the cost of doing business.

For instance, in the electronic production group, the manager should know what the average costs of the pre-production, production, post production and duplication and distribution are for video programs, and develop an overall average cost. The manager of the film production unit should know the average cost of slide production, the unit cost of still photography and the average length of time spent by each photographer on projects. The graphic arts manager should know the average cost per graphics project, and so on.

Each organization must develop whatever cost analysis it needs in order to satisfy its cost-justification program. Cost analysis will prove invaluable from many points of view, one of which is the ability to answer the question, usually posed by novice clients or skeptical management: yes, but how much does it cost? Another reason is that the cost analysis will give media management a control on where costs are increasing or decreasing so that adjustments can be made.

Finally, knowing the costs of the media center just makes good management sense. It provides another way in which media center management can let higher management know that the center is being properly managed. Knowing "the numbers" also provides a basis for giving clients an idea of the scope of a project. For example, a client new to the use of video tape or slides, will appreciate learning that, "The average length of our programming is 15 minutes," or "The average number of slides in a one projector program is usually around 65," and so on. Knowledge of the costs will also give producers, photographers and graphic artists a working idea of how long it should take to complete a particular project, which they can communicate to the client.

REPORTS TO HIGHER MANAGEMENT

Media center management should not wait to be asked "How are things going?" by top management. At regular intervals, media managers should report on the state of the department. For example, monthly reports can be sent to higher management regarding the volume and kind of work being performed, perhaps mentioning the following:

- the number of multimedia programs, video tapes, films, slides, photography assignments and graphics projects produced
- changes in personnel
- additions to hardware
- awards or special commendations received from clients
- out of the ordinary projects or assignments
- special training for media production staffers
- changes in procedures that have improved overall operations
- visits from peers from other organizations

Reports such as these keep the media center in the forefront. They present an aggressive posture that can translate into higher management's perception that the center is being well managed. A periodic report also reminds higher management that the media center is making a valuable contribution to the organization.

The report should occasionally make comparisons such as: how many slide projects were completed in January of this year as compared to last; has the overall volume of photography assignments increased or decreased in the last six months; has there been a shift in the use of video tape from one application to another? Information of this kind can also be used to build a case for future requests. For example, if the volume of video production work is increasing, or the film unit is experiencing an increase in the volume of slide production, the next budget cycle might find media management requesting additional personnel, hardware or operating dollars. The monthly reports can tell higher management that change is taking place and when the request for additional personnel, equipment and operating dollars is formally made, it will not come as a total surprise. Periodic reports will have helped to build up the perception that the requests have a basis in fact, rather than in creative production fancy.

QUALITY CONTROL

Quality control checkpoints should be developed for each aspect of the media production operation. The manager of each unit should be responsible for developing quality control mechanisms. For example, a system can be developed to check on the technical quality of video cassettes before they are shown or distributed to field locations. Even the labels on the video cassettes should be double-checked to make sure they contain the right program name, length, release date and correct spelling of the names of any executives. Similar quality control checks should be exercised on slides, photographs, films and so on. Regardless of the medium involved, some system should be developed so that someone other than the originator of the project has a look at the output to check for technical quality.

THE OPERATIONS MANUAL

Most of the media center's activities should be formalized into an operations manual. The operations manual will provide a new manager with a ready reference as to how things get done, what procedures are used, what policies are followed, and so on. It also serves as a handy reference for anyone working in the department.

At a minimum, the media center operations manual should contain the following information:

- A description of the media center's purpose and objectives
- A specific breakdown of the purpose and objectives of each unit within the media center

- A formal description of all jobs in the operation, including general statements, requirements for the position, job performance expectations and chain of command
- Measures of performance standards—means by which management can evaluate the performance standards set forth in the job descriptions
- The media center's rate card
- A formal organizational chart
- Pertinent organizational policies, such as those regarding vacations, sick leave, holidays, EEO requirement, etc.
- Departmental policies
- Media center policies
- Production procedures—each unit manager may have developed procedures that everyone in the department must follow which should be outlined formally in the manual
- Forms—all the forms used in the department should be in the manual with an explanation as to their use and function
- Lists of frequently used outside vendors, any specific arrangements with these vendors, and copies of contracts
- Formal procedures for using outside vendors
- Statements regarding the use of copyrighted materials

LIBRARIES AND CATALOGS

In time, a media center may develop a sufficient number of graphics, photographic prints, slides, 16mm films, audio tape programs, multimedia programs, video tape programs, and even perhaps video disc programs, to justify the creation of a library. A media library can serve various purposes. In serves as an archival depository for at least one copy of each program the center produces. It makes it possible to retrieve programs to be used again, even years later.

A media library, then, implies a media catalog. Such catalogs are of enormous value, especially if there is a lot of material, and if many different locations within the organization need to use the library. Catalogs could be created for each of the departments within the media center; moreover, each department catalog could be sub-divided by application. For example, a slide library (sometimes called a slibrary) catalog could be divided by communication areas: internal communications and external communications.

7

Marketing the Media Center

PUBLICITY AND PROMOTION

The media center that does a poor job of marketing itself within the organization will have little credibility with organizational clients seeking to enhance their own communications efforts. In addition, the corporate media center serves a function similar to that of external agencies. As an "in-house agency," the center must act to get the organization's attention, and to "sell" its services. Publicity and sales promotion are two ways of accomplishing this.

There are various ways in which an in-house media center can get publicity and promote itself. One obvious way is to get written up in the organization's house organ. A suggested hook for the feature could be "How does an in-house media center serve an organization?" Or it could be a description of a special project. The house organ can also focus on each unit of the department, which means that over a period of time each aspect of the center can be covered in some detail. The house organ is a good place to publicize recently completed projects, or promote existing resources, such as a listing of tapes in the video library, or the center's slide library. Because the media center's output is highly visual, photographs of the operation or of a project in the process of production are a natural. Photos could show the head of the organization making a video tape or a film, how a multimedia production is done, or the development of a storyboard for a slide program. Media production is graphic; it lends itself beautifully to graphic promotion.

The house organ is just one natural publicity outlet in the organizational system. There are others. Bulletin boards, cafeteria spaces, even office elevators can all be used for promotion. Media center management can also use the facility itself as a showcase. Blanks walls can be used to display production shots from various programs. The general access areas can also be used to display awards garnered by the department. These efforts should convey the message that successful and effective work is going on in the media center.

The media department can also garner publicity and promotion indirectly by either soliciting, nurturing or actually writing features on the department for publication in the trade press. Once published, the article can be framed for display, and copies can be forwarded to key management personnel. Depending on the organization, the article may be spotted without it having to be distributed. All the better. It is wise to touch base with upper management to let them know of the press' interest in the operation.

Sales promotion can be done by setting up meetings with key personnel or potential clients who are not familiar with the media center's services. At these meetings, the manager can present clips from video or film programs, show a particularly effective slide presentation, give the client a tour of the facility, introduce production personnel, and so on.

Clients can also be marketed to by individual memo. For example, say the graphics group recently completed the design of a new logo for an existing product. A short memo to the marketing director of another operating division mentioning the new logo might get some attention and generate business.

An essential element of promotion is the development of show reels. Each unit should maintain an up to date promotion reel. Graphics arts should have a portfolio of recent and effective graphics; the film group should be prepared to show various types and styles of slide production work and still photography (both black and white, and color); the electronic media group should have video cassettes showing various styles and applications. The media center might develop an overall applications reel, or separate reels for marketing, training, employee communications, external communications, and so on.

In all, publicity and sales promotion should have the long term effect of generating business and keeping existing clients. Publicity and promotion can also help generate high employee morale, by providing an opportunity for everybody in the unit to get credit for their contributions to the media center. High morale helps improve operations, develop innovative output and thereby keep the media center in business.

MARKETING AND SELLING

The media center is in competition with all external media production agencies. It must seek out clients, and prepare and submit competitive media project proposals. In sum, the in-house media center is a business. As such, the center must be marketed not just once a year when budgets are reviewed, but all the time. The media center manager and the managers of the various units within the center must also be prepared to market and sell their "products," if the center is to remain viable.

It might seem odd that an in-house department should have to take on the marketing stance of an outside agency. Yet it seems that more and more organizations are moving toward decision package analysis techniques; in increasing numbers, organizations are taking the position that staff departments should put a price tag on their services and that these services should price their value by bringing in enough work to pay for themselves. In this kind of climate, media center management must be prepared to adopt a strong marketing and selling attitude.[1]

What follows are some techniques for bolstering the media center's status in the organization by maintaining an aggressive marketing stance:

Know the organization. Successfully selling the media center requires talent, tenacity and good timing. It also requires self-confidence and knowledge—knowledge of clients' communications problems, of the organization's business, its products, customers, employees, and its past, present and future.

Know other organizations. Managers should know how other organizations, especially similar organizations, are using media — what equipment they use, how they are staffed, the kinds of projects they produce, how much each project costs, how heavily they rely on outside vendors, their failures and successes, how they evaluate their projects and how they sell management on media.

Develop media seminars. Show what can be done, let clients respond to examples and let them get involved in the decision making process. Let them teach themselves how effective media can be. Bring in outside experts on media production and bring in managers and personnel from other organizations to tell their stories.

Produce quality work. Nothing is more damaging to a media center's image than a project stamped by its audience as amateur. And while the quality of a project does not necessarily ensure communications effectiveness, lack of it can instantly negate the real value of any content. While this does not mean that every media project has to cost a fortune, it does mean that shortchanging or shaving expenses from the cost of production can only result in a product that reads, sounds and/or looks like it was done on a shoestring budget. The cost of a media project should not only be cost-effective, it should also reflect the quality of professionalism all clients expect.

Project a professional attitude. Clients want assurance that they are dealing with professionals. This means understanding the advantages (and disadvantages) of the various media, asking informed questions, being organized, following up, etc.

Get out of the office and promote. Take the initiative. Find out who could use the center the most. Which departments have the most need? Who in management is most disposed to the use of media? Ask for a 15-minute interview, and let it be the first of several.

Take advantage of chance. Make the unexpected work to advantage. A chance meeting in the corridor with a member of management who mentions he's having a communications problem could turn into an opportunity for a media project. Be alert to those opportunities.

Followup. A casual suggestion to a prospective client can be turned into a media project only if the client has something he or she can look at in black and white. Follow up informal suggestions with a written proposal. Keep it short and to the point.

Learn to say no. This means taking charge. Let clients understand that if they want the right results, there is a proper way of getting them. Remember, the media center wouldn't have clients if the center weren't staffed with experts. If the client was the expert, in-house media professionals would not have jobs.

Demonstrate and educate. Show client A what was done for Client B (and vice versa). Show other clients what was done for clients A and B. And show all of them what other organizations are doing. A picture is still worth a thousand words.

Develop a mailing list. Who in the organization is involved in using media? The basic idea of a mailing list is to keep people informed. Make them feel part of an effective communications system.

Distribute pertinent literature. Forward copies of appropriate articles on media to select clients. Summarize the results of pertinent studies. Compare studies findings to the organization's use of media. Communicate this information.

Use innovation sparingly. Tried and true methods may be old hat to you, but to a new client this translates into: "I understand what you're suggesting." Use innovative techniques only when they contribute to solving the client's communications needs. To paraphrase the design philosophy of architect Frank Lloyd Wright, let the form and technique of the media project grow out of needs of the client and the project's content.

Ask for written testimonials. If a media project is a special success, ask the client for a written testimonial. Make copies of it and send at least one copy to higher management in the form of an FYI. Keep a "testimonial" file and review it at least once every three months. The file will be a terrific confidence builder; it will also enhance the center's reputation with management.

Initiate the second sale. So you just finished a project for a new client. Is that the end of it? Perhaps that first project can turn into a series of projects, or a follow-up program in three, six, or even twelve months later. In short, always keep long-term interests in mind.

Cross-sell. Banks like to sell a checking account customer a savings account, or vice versa. Similarly, in the corporate media business, you can sell clients on various applications. Just because a client uses video for training purposes does not mean he or she could not also use it for management communications.

Use existing publicity outlets. Let's say you just finished producing the company's update of a five-year old orientation program. If you took photos of the production in progress and shots of the program itself, get them published in the company house organ. Make posters using scenes from the program. Ask local employee relations personnel to display the posters.

Formally evaluate programs. Sooner or later management will want to know if the projects they paid for did what they were supposed to do (presuming that objectives were defined). Don't wait to be asked. Have an evaluation procedure designed before production starts. Summarize the results, and communicate them to the client and other managers who could benefit from the feedback (e.g., using the mailing list you developed earlier).

Confront the stubborn ones. When you've developed a sufficient number of ongoing clients, and the number of projects has increased, confront potential clients who initially gave you a negative response. In effect, ask, "What do I have to do to get your business?" Sometimes the answer to this question will reveal a misconception — about various media, about the media center, about production costs, about their access to the center's expertise. Use this opportunity to change a prospective client's attitude.

Track the center's progress. At least once every six months, list all management and production activities; then summarize them. Let management know how far the media center has come. Not only does it serve to substantiate the center's growing reputation with immediate management, it also provides a quick picture of the extent of media use within the organization. One of the advantages of working in the organizational media business is that no one customer dominates the use of media. The center should have many clients from various parts of the organization, if media center management has done a good job selling. So, while immediate management might perceive that the use of media is low (because they use media infrequently), it may in fact be extensive! A summary of programs and clients will help change this perception.

Be aggressive during economic hard times. There is a tendency in organizations during times of economic uncertainty for management to pull back and take a more conservative attitude toward plans, projects and policies. Whether the economic uncertainty is real or imagined, mild or severe, what counts is the "perception" of the uncertainty. Don't be put in the position of losing business when the organizational mood may be over-reacting to the situation. Maintain an aggressive attitude, despite the impulse to become conservative along with everyone else.

Look for more business. Suddenly, department budgets for communications are reduced by 15%. In this economic environment the media center cannot afford to "wait it out." If the media center stands still, it may find that its clientele has dried up completely. Managers should draw up an extensive, detailed list of potential user clients: marketing, training, safety, corporate communications, environmental affairs, consumer affairs, financial analyst relations, production, personnel, medical, quality control, etc. Put the list of potential customers in rank order. List as first those who would be the most likely candidates to use media and so on, down the line. Then decide on a timetable: month number 1, contact all training departments; month number 2, contact marketing departments, etc.

Put your best cost-effective foot forward. Managers should know the average length of programming, average costs of production, average cost of post-production, average duplication costs and average duplication run size. Managers should also have a firm idea of year to year aggregate costs and be ready with hard numbers in answer to hard economic questions.

Develop a marketing package. Develop promotional material. A natural, of course, is a short five to ten minute video promotional piece on the center: what you do, what you've produced, how you do it, with what results, etc. A print piece is also useful for wider distribution. And don't forget natural publicity outlets, like the company house organ, publications designed for special interest groups (e.g., safety directors) and local plant publications. Consider the media center's physical surroundings as part of the marketing package. What does the center's environment say about how you do business, how professionally you do it and with what success? Here you might use photographs on the walls of the office or reception area to show off past successes and, of course, a display of awards won for media excellence. The style of the marketing package says something about the media center — it indicates the professionalism of the center's production techniques and the success of its programs.

FOOTNOTES

1. Some portions of this chapter are adapted, with permission, from Eugene Marlow, "Defending Against the Recession," *Videography,* February 1980, and Eugene Marlow, "The Sale of Video Begins When Management Says 'No'," *Videography,* November 1977, Copyright United Business Publications, Inc.

8

Working with Executives, Clients and Experts

The success or failure of a media center can greatly depend on the quality of interpersonal relationships between media center personnel, on the one hand, and executives, clients and subject experts on the other. In many ways, media center operations are people intensive. There are dozens of situations in which media center staff interact with executives, clients and experts: during pre-production meetings, script reviews, storyboard sessions, video and film shoots, editing sessions, program reviews, budget reviews, problem-definition meetings, photography sessions, and more. It is important, therefore, that every member of the media center staff be aware of the dynamics that can occur between themselves and others. It is essentially a matter of handling conflicts; conflicts that occur in various ways.

In order to analyze the kinds of conflicts that can occur and ways in which media center personnel can handle these, I will describe a scene. This scene is the rehearsal of a management communications video tape session.

SCENE — THE REHEARSAL

10 am The technical crew has been at work since 8:30. The video engineer has been adjusting the cameras for an hour. The director has made last minute adjustments to the lighting with one of the technicians. The producer is reviewing his pre-production notes. This morning's video

recording will be used to help participants improve their on-camera performance and the program's structure and content. The subject of the program is energy conservation. The participants include the company's director of energy conservation, a corporate vice president in charge of energy supplies and materials services, and ... the company president. Of the three, only the company president has been on television before.

10:05 am A representative from the public affairs department walks in. He chats with the producer about the pre-production meeting of two weeks ago. He is nervous. He smokes two cigarettes in five minutes.

10:16 am Nervous frowns turn to nervous smiles. The president and the others arrive. The rehearsal begins. The producer greets the president with a handshake:

"Warren."

"How long are you going to keep me under the hot lights?"

"Not long. We should have you out of here in about 45 minutes. Warren, would you sit here at the far end of the table. You'll be talking into that camera for your introduction and close. Jim and Bruce — would you please sit on the long side here, and here."

Bruce B., the energy conservation director, a man 6′ 3″ tall, hesitatingly asks, "Should I be looking at the camera, or speaking to Warren and Jim?"

The producer replies, "Your instincts are right. You should all be having a conversation with one another. The audience knows that this has been rehearsed and structured. They take that for granted. You know what you want to say. Warren, did you get that list of questions to ask Bruce and Jim, and the opening and close?"

"Yes, but I haven't had a chance to read them yet."

"Why don't you take a moment now to look them over."

The vice president asks the producer, "What do I do about my very obvious, uh, uh, Southern accent?"

The vice president also has a stutter. The producer replies, "Well, your accent is a part of you and you seem to have done well with it for a long time. Don't worry about it. Be yourself. That's the best thing."

10:31 am The executive cast finally settles down. Tape rolls. The director instructs the man on camera one to signal the president to begin his introduction. The president doesn't quite see it, despite the instructions given him earlier. He finally sees it on a third try.

The first run-through is dull and stiff. All three executives have misconceptions about how to act on television. They pose, they don't move their bodies, they look serious all the time. They do stick to the script's structure, though, which is positive. All the pre-production work has paid off in that respect.

10:55 am The first rehearsal is over. The lights are shut off. The cast looks a bit perturbed. They don't know what to think of their performance. The director quickly rewinds the video cassette. He hands the cassette to the producer who puts it into a video player. He pushes the play button and watches intently with the rest of the cast. He says nothing through the playback of the first few minutes. The president looks at the producer with a puzzled look.

"Well, what do you think?" the producer asks.

The president breaks the ice. "I think we need to loosen up."

A sigh is let out that is heard around the world. The two other executives willingly agree. The producer supports the conclusion. "Of course, the first time through is always the hardest. Everybody who has ever been on television goes through the same thing. The first time I saw myself on the tube, I thought, 'My god, is that me, is that what I look like, sound like?' "

The producer observes morer relaxation on the collection of faces. "Frankly, though, I will say that I don't think we need to make any changes in the content or structure. It plays out very well." The public affairs representative readily agrees. He suggests two minor structural changes in the body of the vice president's text. There is much agreement. The producer jumps in to initiate the second run-through before there are any more suggestions for minor changes.

11:13 am The second rehearsal commences. It is much better, tighter. The cast is more relaxed. The vice president's stutter is far less pronounced. the president relates anecdotes to make the link between corporate energy conservation and energy conservation in the home. It is much more believable and human.

The second run-through ends at 11:30 am. The producer quickly plays back the second tape. They only watch the first five minutes. Everyone can see the improvement. Lots of smiling faces around the room.

11:37 am Confirmation of the meeting place and time for the shoot tomorrow. The president and others leave. After a few closing words with the public affairs representative, the producer sits down for a de-briefing with the technical crew. "We will probably shoot it in one take tomorrow," he says.

WHAT HAPPENED?

Identifying the "Teams"

Rehearsing executives for a management communications video program provides an opportunity to analyze some inherent conflicts between "management" and "functional" rank.

In the scene described above, there were various "players" present.*
First is the producer. This individual is usually not of high managerial
rank. In relation to the rest of the characters at the rehearsal, the producer
stands above the technical crew (production engineer, director and the two
camera persons) in managerial rank, but below the corporate executives.

On the other side is the public affairs department representative. This
individual has more status than the producer primarily because he more
often interacts with highly placed executives. Several notches above the
public affairs representative is the director of energy conservation, who, in
turn, reports to the corporate vice president in charge of energy supplies
and materials services. The president, of course, is highest in rank among
all the performers in this scene.

Thus, there are essentially two teams in this drama. The producer and
the technical crew are on one team; the president and the other executives
are on the other, along with the public affairs representative.

Although the producer ostensibly belongs to the former team, he must
also serve as the single member of a third team; that of ombudsman
between the two teams. Therefore, the producer may play with the
technical crew, but he may also have to play with the other team when
appropriate, or alone, when necessary.

Analying and Resolving Conflicts

From the outset, the scene is fraught with conflict. To begin with, the
unstated but obvious conflict is (1) the differentiation between the
managerial rank of the president's team and the producer's team, and (2)
the "functional" ranking of the two teams. The producer's team may be low
in rank, relatively speaking, in terms of managerial authority, but the
president's team is completely outranked by the producer's team in terms
of the skills required to perform successfully at the video rehearsal.

Thus, the president's team is put into the functional role of students —
they don't know what to do in the rehearsal. The producer's team, on the
other hand, is well versed on what goes on during a rehearsal; they have
done it before with many other executives for similar kinds of programs.
However, only the producer has the skills necessary to guide the technical
crew and the president's team through the experience. Therefore, the
producer must directly play the role of teacher.

---

*The dramaturgical analogies used in this analysis are borrowed from Erving
Goffman's book, *The Presentation of Self in Everyday Life* (New York:
Doubleday/Anchor, 1959.)

Despite this inherent conflict, the motivation for both teams in this scene is ostensibly the same: to perform well at the rehearsal and to achieve a future performance that will be both belivable and successful. However, there are variations on how each team achieves this objective. The producer's team must do all it can to ensure a technically successful rehearsal; i.e. properly focused lights, even audio-levels, smooth camera work, properly timed cuts between cameras. The producer's task is to upgrade the performance of the president's team without overstepping the bounds of rank or personally insulting any of the president's team players. The president's team members, on the other hand, must maintain the semblance of managerial authority and skill (in this case, communication skills) associated with high rank, while at the same time maintaining continuity of program structrue and content. Moreover, there is an added conflict in the president's team: they wish to know how to perform better in the unknown rehearsal situation, but cannot, in most cases, bring themselves to directly ask: "What should I do?"

It is debatable which team experiences the greater pressure. Perhaps the home team has a slight advantage. Not only does the producer's team have the psychological advantage of technical skills, but it also knows the actual physical territory. The president's team must not only quickly acclimate to the new performance situation, but must also rapidly adjust to the unfamiliar, physical environment.

The conflict between managerial and functional rank is even more pronounced during the rehearsal. There is an inherent conflict as a result of varying degrees of skill; also, the learning of the skill is very public. Even though the public is relatively small (the technical crew, the producer, the public affairs representative and the members of the president's team), each member of the president's team must impress the others by giving a good performance — and the successful performance must be done in the present, the here and now! A bad performance cannot be hidden. The president, too, must perform successfully, if he is to maintain his reputation.

Although his performance will not appear on video tape in front of a large audience, the producer's success is contingent on the successful performance of the president's team. The public affairs representative, however, has a couple of "play options." If the producer's actions result in a poor performance on the part of the president's team, he can always opt to say, "Perhaps we should have gone to a more professional organization to get this done," or "Video communications is too risky, let's try something else to comunicate our message." If the performances are successful, he can opt to say, "I knew this would turn out well."

The rehearsal is an intriguing situation. Not only is it a means of improving one's future performance; it is also in itself a meaningful performance. As students of playwriting know, a good play is one in which there is a conflict and one in which one or more of the characters change in some way. In the rehearsal the essential conflict is between managerial and functional rank. And in more ways than one, if the producer performs well, the president's team members will leave the rehearsal changed: they will have become better performers, at least in front of the camera.

TECHNIQUES

The rehearsal for a video communications program is only one common situation in which executives, clients or subject experts come in contact with the media center staff. Let us look at some other potential conflicts the media center staff may encounter.

Handling the Communications Novice

A subject expert or client walks into a producer's office and declares: "I want to produce a video tape. Can you help me?" If you probe the expert at this point, you'll find that he or she (especially if this is his or her first video production) is probably scared to death just walking into the office. Why? Video is a sophisticated electronic communications tool. Lacking knowledge of how video works or how it should be approached can be highly intimidating. The expert will probably try to maintain as much control of the situation (i.e., the production) as possible to keep from showing the fear he or she is probably experiencing. What should you do?[1]

- At the beginning, let the client or expert do the talking. He or she may feel the need to convince the producer of his or her expertise. Be patient. The client or expert comes to the media center with needs, not vice versa.

- Initially, avoid using too many technical terms. Converse in the client's language. Ask for definitions — people love to talk about what they know. The more he or she talks about the familiar, the more comfortable and confident the client will become. Ask questions about the expert's background. The more one knows about this person as a person, the more one will be able to deal with the expert on a personal level.

- Be patient. Convincing others that you know what you are doing takes time. No one likes to have totally new ideas thrust upon them at once and be expected to act on those concepts immediately. Let the client or expert assimilate your credentials slowly. You'll reach your objective faster.

- Be yourself. While it may appear that some people have become successful because they were the epitome of perfection, people prefer to deal with someone who is human, genuine and at ease with himself.

- When dealing with clients, ignore *what* they are, and concentrate on *who* they are. Clients want to know they are dealing with a professional, especially one who is not intimidated by rank.

- There is a need to reach a clear agreement about expectations concerning when and how things get done. If a client's expectations are too high — given the time, manpower and financial resources available — they must be lowered. Conversely, if they are too low —because of concern about the center's abilities or fear that the production process will be an agonizing one — then those expectations must also be changed before the process goes too far.

- Give the clients what they need, not what they want. Sometimes clients ask for or expect things by expressing them as vague notions or stubborn demands. Sometimes a client will want something that is inappropriate; at times a statement is made in a video program, or article or speech draft, that upon later review is irrelevant or extraneous. Some clients may insist that their every "pearl of wisdom" remain, but common sense may dictate that the statement should come out. If the project is to be successful, an audience other than the client will have to receive it. Media center staffs have an obligation to the client's audience to take out extraneous material.

- Clients, especially those uninformed about the media production process, are occasionally eager to show you how much they know about producing. They feel they have to maintain command of the situation and begin the discussion by describing their ideas for script, set, graphics, metaphors, etc. While an immediate reaction could be to ask about the client's objectives and audiences, a useful riposte to this kind of client is to say "Well, before we start discussing style, let's talk about content; that is, what needs to be said, the order in which it has to be said, and who will say it." This can be an effectively disarming technique.

- Be selective as to when, and how involved, a client gets in the production process. A client does not have to be involved in every step. In my experience, it is a rare client who will take as strong an interest in the production process as media staffs. However, because the large majority of clients are members of management, it is to their advantage that the time they spend in the production process be used effectively and efficiently. While the client should not become as totally immersed in the production as you, the client should still have opportunities to contribute to the program. However, if the suggested contribution is inappropriate, this should be made known, and reasons given. Again, what a client thinks is needed may not support his or her objectives, and these suggestions must be dealt with immediately.

- Keep the situation informal and unfettered by bureaucratic requirements. Good humor is a must. Minimize the amount of paper work generated during the production process. Program proposals and budgets can be effective even when they are short. Schedules do not have to be complicated to be useful. Program evaluations do not have to be two inches thick in order to prove that the program achieved its objectives.

- Maintain a relationship with a client even after project completion. If the program was successful, the client will be back for more. Success breeds success and the best form of advertisement is a satisfied client. This kind of promotion lays the foundation for a smooth process with future potential clients.

Basically, in handling clients, one often uses the proven techniques of salesmanship. First, you have to sell yourself. But you really cannot do that until you know something about the customer, here, media center clients. Once you have laid the foundation you can begin to sell your expertise, and thus, reach the ultimate objective: satisfying the client's needs while meeting the audience's demands.

All in all, the best way to ensure that a media project is shepherded efficiently from conception to completion is to develop a client's respect for the media center's talents and expertise. It is that simple. The more trust and confidence a client has in the center's skill and experience, the more likely the project will be successful, because the easier it will be to do what professionalism dictates should be done. Trust in the center's abilities will provide for greater flexibility in scheduling, making changes and explaining why something didn't get done when planned. Creating this trust is the difference between a center that is merely competent and one that is very successful.

FOOTNOTES

1. Some portions of this chapter are adapted, with permission from Marlow, Eugene, "Handling the Expert," *Videography,* March 1977, Copyright United Business Publications, Inc.

9

Using External Resources

Striking an appropriate balance between an organization's use of in-house and external resources is a fundamental key to the effectiveness of a corporate media center. Media center managers should use external resources when appropriate, and coordinate these resources with in-house capabilities. In my experience external resources are indispensable, no matter how advanced the center is. Often, the more work an in-house operation does, the more it tends to use external resources.[1]

OUTSIDE RESOURCES TO CONSIDER

The following is a list of the types of external resources a media center may consider using:

Consultants

organizational communication systems consultants
graphic design consultants
film production consultants
video production consultants
audiovisual facilities design consultants
talent agencies

photographic facilities design consultants
video production facilities design consultants
teleconference facilities design consultants
video disc programming consultants

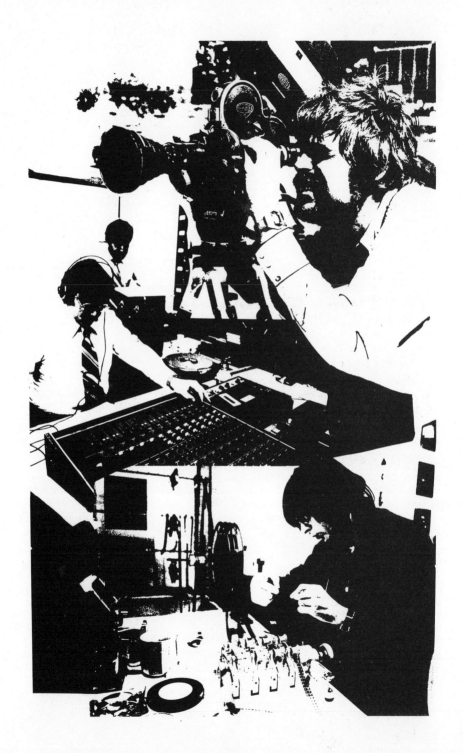

Production facilities

typography services	audio tape post-production
print duplication production	audio tape duplication
photography re-touching and color correction	audio tape mixing
film editing facilities (16mm and 35mm film)	equipment rental (for camera, lights, etc.)
film laboratories	slide duplication
film duplication (super 8mm, 16mm and 35mm)	multimedia production
	slide-to-film transfers
film (audio track) mixing	slide-to-tape transfers
film animation stand production	film-to-tape transfers
	tape-to-film transfers
video production	16mm film to super 8mm film duplication
video post-production	multimedia to video tape transfers
video tape duplication	
audio production	multimedia to film transfer

Production houses

A production house differs from a production facility in that it provides the creative staff, along with — but not always — the production facility.

graphic production	multimedia production
film production	audio production
slide production	photography production
video production	

Freelancers

art directors	maintenance engineers/technicians
graphic designers	
mechanical artists	print copywriters
photographers	film scriptwriters
cinematographers	video scriptwriters
directors of photography	multimedia production scriptwriters
lighting directors	
producers	video disc programming scriptwriters
directors	
audio recordists	on-camera professional talent

voice-over professional talent
models
film animation/photoanima-
   tion designers
film editors
video editors
video engineers
audio engineers
production assistants
technical directors

camera persons (video)
researchers
administrative assistants
music editors
stage managers
audiovisual technicians
grips and gaffers
makeup artists
set designers
costume designers

Canned materials

music and sound effects
canned films
canned video programming
film stock shots

video stock shots
slide libraries
canned multimedia programming
picture (graphic) libraries

Supplies

paper
pens, brushes, and pentels
photographic paper
audio tape
video tape

positive and negative 16mm and
   35mm film
mag track (for film production)
bulbs
equipment parts
photographic chemicals

Equipment (hardware) suppliers

graphic storage
graphic design tables
still photography cameras
photographic processing
slide production stands
slide duplication
cinemagraphic equipment
video cameras
video editing

video tape recorders
film projectors
audio recording and mixing
   equipment
lighting equipment
video tape duplication
distribution amplifiers
film recording
audio mixing

CRITERIA FOR SELECTING EXTERNAL RESOURCES

The organization or media manager must have some criteria for selecting external resources, and these will vary depending on the specific resources involved. Below are some suggested criteria for each external resource mentioned.

Consultants

What criteria can the organization use for determining which consultant is the best for the job? Here are a few:

How many years of experience does the consultant have?
Does he or she have a successful track record?
Has the consultant worked for one kind of organization, or for organizations in different industries?
What is the consultant's reputation in the industry and with former clients?
What kind of organization does the consultant have?
Is the consultant willing to present proposals prepared for other clients (provided the material is not proprietary)?
What is the consultant's operating philosophy?
Is he or she open to new ideas, or willing to apply new technologies?
Will the consultant work well with others in the organization?
Does the consultant have an inquiring mind?
Is the consultant willing to listen to others, and is he or she flexible?
Is the consultant familiar with the work of other leading consultants in the field?
What kind of professional organizations does the consultant belong to?
Is the consultant available when needed?
Is the consultant's fee structure competitive?
Does the consultant communicate ideas clearly and succinctly? Both verbally and in writing?
Is the consultant willing to prepare a written proposal?

Production Facilities

With respect to production facilities, the following questions are crucial:

What kind of equipment does the facility have, and is it well-maintained?
Is the equipment up-to-date or state-of-the-art?
Is the equipment serviced by a professional staff?

What is the facility's reputation with existing customers?

How long have they been in business?

Does the facility have a reputation for a high level of service and cooperation?

What is the facility's availability?

What is the facility's overall level of quality?

What is the facility's price structure? Is it competitive?

Who are its clients?

Does the pricing schedule match the level of quality and service?

Production Houses

When choosing production houses, the following criteria might be applied:

How well acquainted is the production house with quality production facilities in the area?

How long has the production house been in business?

Does it specialize in one kind of application (such as marketing, public relations, etc.)?

What is its reputation with clients?

What kinds of organizations has it worked for in the past?

What is its style of production?

Does the production house have a reputation for producing programming that is on time, within budget and meets objectives?

Does it have a systems approach to media programming, or is it more interested in producing programming that is merely aesthetically pleasing?

How well will production house personnel work with in-house clients, subject experts or executives?

Is their price schedule competitive?

How many examples of previous work is the production house representative willing to show?

What kind of staff does the production house have?

What is the depth of experience of the production house principals and staff?

Does the production house have a successful track record?

What is the production house's reputation in the industry?

Has the production house been written up in trade publications?

What is the production house's operating philosophy?

Is the production house open to new ideas, or does it use old formulas?

Does the staff have a businesslike approach as well as a creative style?

What standards of quality does the production house adhere to?

Is the production house staff willing to listen to others?

Is the production house familiar with the work of leading houses in the area, and with the work of leading organizational practitioners in the field?

Is the production house staff flexible?

Is the production house available when needed?

Does the production house principal communicate ideas clearly and succinctly?

Is the production house willing to present the organization with production ideas, budgets and schedules, in writing?

Freelancers

Many of the same questions posed to consultants, production facilities and production houses could be asked of freelancers. In addition, for supplies and equipment, price, warranties and service are important criteria for selection. For example, if the external resource is a dealer in photographic or video equipment, the organization should question the dealer's ability and reputation with respect to delivery date commitments. The organization should also be concerned about the dealer's willingness and reputation to fulfill waranty commitments.

Bidding and purchasing

Pricing, of course, is an important consideration. Other things being equal, organizations should use a bid procedure when selecting an outside vendor, especially when equipment or supplies are involved. However, there will be times when the lowest priced vendor may not necessarily be the best external resource for equipment and supplies. The organization has to examine the vendor's reputation, delivery record and service reputation. All these criteria together will determine whether the vendor will be given a contract. The organization's purchasing department should get involved, particularly when the external resource involves capital equipment and supplies. In these instances in particular an organization's purchasing function may have more clout in obtaining the right price and delivery schedule than the media center will.

Organizational purchasing functions can also get involved in hiring consulting, production facility or production house services. However, in these instances the purchasing function may serve more in an administrative capacity. The role of the purchasing function in these cases will differ from one organization to another. It should be underlined, however, that the purchasing function can be a useful ally regardless of the service being purchased, either before, during or after the service has been provided. In many cases, the purchasing function can serve the media center well by helping to draw up purchasing contracts that protect the organization, while at the same time providing the external resources needed.

The presentation

A marketing presentation by the external resource being considered may be a clue to the resource's desirability. An external resource can "pitch" itself through a print piece, a phone call, an on-site presentation, a visit by a representative or a combination of the above.

Quality

I have received presentations from hundreds of consultants, production facilities, production houses, freelancers and hardware suppliers. In general, the good suppliers differentiate themselves in several ways.

The first is quality: an in-house organizational client once told me that the first level of success is to perform a job effectively; does the product do what it is supposed to do? Now, if that effective job is also done efficiently (i.e., on time, and within budget) then you are really exemplary. Thus, the first point to consider is the quality of the external resources' wares. How do you judge quality? Here are some criteria:

Is the level of quality consistent, or does it vary from one job to another?

Does the effectiveness of the media presentation reach you on an emotional level?

Do you feel that this vendor is interested in trying just a little harder than the next guy?

Would you be proud to show this vendor's wares to others?

Do you feel the vendor is professional?

Of course, the question of what is quality and what is not is sometimes a matter of taste. There are, however, certain technical ways of judging quality, such as:

Are the colors in the print piece true, and in register?

Is the layout busy or clear?

Is the presentation clear and understandable?

Is the photography fuzzy or sharp?

Is the quality of the film grainy or sharp?

Are the graphics telegraphic or do you have to search the piece to begin to understand what you are looking at?

Is the quality of the audio track understandable, does it make creative use of music, sound effects, voiceovers?

Is the quality of the video picture sharp, and well lit? Is the camerawork creative or dull? Smooth or jerky?

Is the quality of the editing jarring or smooth, and in keeping with the content of the program?

Style

In addition to the technical quality of the vendor's product, the style of the presentation is also a criteria for selection. In my experience, the most successful presentations were those that were simple, well-organized and short. The vendor representative did not try to overwhelm me with credentials, but gave just enough information to whet my appetite for more. The best presentations by production houses, consultants and freelancers have been those where the presentation of product was both broad and short. In other words, I was presented with a variety of products, each of which was a small part of the total product (as opposed to being asked to sit through a 30 to 40 minute film on a subject that had nothing to do with my clients). The question of variety is especially important. If an outside vendor shows up with only one or two examples of work, this vendor should be suspect.

Careful analysis

The better outside resources, consultants in particular, are those who will not be stampeded into giving a price at the presentation. They may, however, be willing to talk about rates, or ball-park figures. The better resources will always ask to have more details about a particular project before committing themselves to a price. In my view, this attitude says several things. First, the vendor is not willing to give his product away; he is not desperate. That reflects a certain level of confidence. Second, this attitude usually shows that the vendor is willing to spend some time working out the details of a particular project. In the long run, this usually means a higher level of quality and service.

Price

The lowest-priced vendor is not necessarily synonymous with poor service, performance or product. The reverse is also true: high price does not guarantee high quality. For example, video tape editing ranges from $100 to $300 an hour. Scriptwriters can charge anything ranging from $100 to $300 or more a finished minute. Directors can cost from $250 a day to almost $1000. Freelance photographers can charge from $250 a day to over $500 a day. The more professional external resources will be willing to submit fairly detailed price breakdowns, as well as schedules of performance.

WHEN TO USE EXTERNAL RESOURCES

External resources should and will be used most of the time, no matter what the size, scope or level of media production activity. Even if the media center operation consists of three people — one graphic artist, one photographer and one video producer/director — all three will require supplies in order to perform their respective functions. At the other extreme, a larger media center — three graphic and mechanical artists, a six-person photography unit, a nine-person electronic media function —will very likely be in constant need of external resources such as consultants, production facilities, production houses, freelancers, supplies, canned materials and hardware vendors.

The trick to using outside resources effectively is matching the right kind of external resource at the right time for the right project at the right price, together with internal resources (while at the same time charging the organization a reasonable price for services rendered by the internal production resource). The combination of the two resources — internal and external — should at one and the same time provide the organization with cost-effective media production services, while keeping the in-house operation competitive; i.e., cost-effective.

To a certain degree, the decision to use external resources may have to be made on a project-by-project basis. External resources will come into play at different times for different reasons (such as when the in-house operation expands and more media execution is accomplished in-house). Therefore, each external resource will be discussed in turn.

Consultants

Consultants can be used at various times in the development of a media center. For example, if an organization is about to change its headquarters location, reorganize, change its product line, change its pricing structure, or revamp its internal or external communications activities, consultants can be called in to help develop ways of effecting this change. Here, media production consultants can be very useful, especially if they have a broad range of production experience (beware of production consultants who have never gotten their hands dirty, technically speaking). Facilities design consultants should be called in if hardware equipment and/or facilities are going to be considered, installed, revamped or changed from one system to another (such as from video tape to video disc playback). Experienced consultants should always be called in if a new technology is under consideration, even if in-house personnel are knowledgeable about it and are well prepared to use it. The consultant in this instance serves as a sounding board and provides a knowledge of other organizations experiences against which the organization can judge its own potential use of the technology.

Production Facilities

There are several instances when a media center should use outside production facilities. The most obvious is when the organization has no media production facilities of its own. Outside production facilities should also be used if the volume of media production is not high enough to warrant the installation of in-house production equipment. Another reason for using outside production facilities is when the external facility has state-of-the-art equipment that the in-house media production organization can not purchase because its frequency of use is not high enough. In some cases, the volume of in-house work is so high that overflow must be handled at an outside facility. Finally, scheduling conflicts and deadlines sometimes make it necessary for work to be performed at an outside facility.

Production Houses

Many of the reasons for using production facilities apply equally to using production houses. If an organization has no in-house media production talent, then an outside production house must be considered. Moreover, if the volume of media production work is not constant or high enough for organizational management to consider hiring creative or technical talent, then outside media production houses should again be considered.

Even when an organization has in-house creative and technical staff, outside production houses may be more up-to-date, since they are in contact with many organizations. This contact requires the production house to be not only competitive, but also up-to-date in order to remain so. Production houses can be useful when the volume of work is so high that in-house staff cannot handle the overflow. Media production schedule conflicts may force the use of outside production houses. An additional reason for using outside production houses is when the nature of a project is such that the in-house staff is not positioned to handle it. For example, the in-house media production group may be organized to effectively and efficiently handle media production that is daily, weekly or even monthly, but some projects may be long-range and require extensive traveling. While an in-house representative may be designated to oversee the project, an outside production house may prove more cost-effective in the long run.

Freelancers

Freelancers should be used almost constantly, no matter how large or small the media production operation. Again, drawing from my own experience, the more professional the in-house media center, the more extensive the use of freelancers.

In sum, the basic reasons for using production facilities and production houses apply equally to freelancers:

- When the organization has no in-house creative or technical media production talent.
- When the volume of work is not sufficiently high to warrant the hiring of in-house creative or technical media production talent.
- When the in-house staff is not as up-to-date or professional.
- When the volume of work is so high the in-house staff cannot handle that work.
- When in-house scheduling conflicts necessitate the use of freelancers.

There are several other times when it proves more cost-effective to use freelancers. In certain instances freelancers are more cost-effective than in-house staff. Here, an important criterion is volume. If, for example, the organization only occasionally originates graphics, photography, films or video programs, freelancers will prove more cost-effective. Similarly, there are certain production functions that do not occur on a frequent basis. For example, unless an organization is producing video programs by the hundreds every year, it does not pay to have camera persons on staff. The same holds true for film editors, lighting designers and makeup artists.

Freelance scriptwriters present an interesting situation. I have found that it is not only more cost-effective to use freelance writers, but also more communications-effective. Most media centers do not have scriptwriters on staff; this function usually falls to the producer/director, who is often handling several media projects as well. Therefore, making use of a freelance scriptwriter frees the in-house producer/director, allowing him or her to be more productive. Moreover, other things being equal, if the producer/director were to figure out the cost of his or her time to write a script, freelance scriptwriters might be less expensive. Finally, no one scriptwriter can effectively write for all kinds of communications applications. Some writers are more adept at writing marketing programs than training programs, and vice versa. With the advent of the video disc the difference in scriptwriting expertise among various applications will become even more pronounced.

Canned Materials

Canned materials present an obvious opportunity for the organization to save money. Implicit in the term "canned" is the idea that the material has already been produced; the organization does not have to originate the material. There are a myriad of companies that have produced video tapes and films on a variety of subjects. The availability of canned programming does not preclude an organization from originating its own material, of course. It may even modify canned programming, provided that the organization receives written permission from the program originator.

Canned media elements, such as music and stock shots, can be found through media libraries and contribute to original programming. When using canned materials, it is important to obey the copyright laws. The originator of the material presumes it will be used in accordance with copyright law.

Hardware and Supplies

Once an organization decides to initiate, install and develop a media center, it needs to develop relationships with outside hardware and supplies vendors. This is true for small, medium and large centers.

External resources are an essential part of the organizational media center operation. The question of when external resources come into play depends very heavily on (1) the volume of media production work, and (2) the professionalism, and thus, cost-effectiveness, of in-house creative and technical staff.

DEALING WITH EXTERNAL RESOURCES

These are some additional pointers to keep in mind when dealing with external resources.

Don't wait until you need a vendor to find one. Check out the availability of vendors in your area. Know who to call on in an emergency. Get to know the best vendors in your area. Keep a file and review it from time to time. Take nothing for granted: if a vendor looks good, check out his credentials. Ask other organizations what kind of service the vendor provides. Keep the file up to date. You may be satisfied with your current vendor pool, but continue to meet new ones to keep the pool fresh.

Don't put all outside needs in one vendor basket. No single vendor can satisfy all outside needs. Segment your needs. For example, it may be less expensive to use an outside production facility, hire a freelance writer for the script, and another freelancer to produce and direct it. Using different vendors for hardware and software might also help bring costs down.

Don't expect miracles. Most outside suppliers who survive the market-place survive because they are good and they have something to offer. However, they are just as susceptible to having problems and making mistakes as those who are part of the in-house operation. Moreover, working with an outside vendor may mean working just as hard to get what is needed as working with in-house resources.

Demand quality. People usually only give what they perceive others will demand of them. Ergo, outside vendors will usually only provide that level of quality they think you will expect. Demand quality and good outside vendors will respond. Sometimes, challenging vendors to perform at a higher level than expected proves fruitful not only for the organization but also for the outside vendor as well.

Let good vendors know you appreciate their work. Outside vendors are not the enemy. If they do a good job, let them know it (and if they don't, let them know that too, even when it's an exception). Everyone needs feedback, both positive and negative. All that is needed is a phone call or a short note. Either way, effective relationships with outside vendors (just like with in-house clients) need to be cultivated. Sharing feedback is one way.

Confirm agreements in writing. No matter how longstanding a relationship with an outside vendor, confirm agreements in writing. The legal department does not need to get into the act every time you call up a supplier for a box of video cassettes. But it does mean that a confirmation of the work to be performed should be in writing in some form. A good outside vendor will do this as a matter of course. Many organizations require an outside vendor to supply a written estimate as a check against actual charges. Something in writing up front helps answer a lot of questions later.

Pay vendors on time. A paid vendor is a happy vendor. Just imagine if the organization didn't pay in-house personnel on time!

Trust your vendor. Once you've established an ongoing relationship with an outside supplier, trust him or her. If you're constantly calling to find out if the script is finished or if the shipment of tapes has left the warehouse, you will only create an unnecessarily tense situation. If you don't feel the vendor will give you the kind of service you want without constant double-checking, find a vendor who will.

Learn your vendor's business. Ask vendors questions about how they do what they do for you. Understand their problems while they try to solve yours. Become fluent with the terms of each vendor's profession. In-house personnel often turn to outside suppliers for help with a problem, and therefore must be able to communicate effectively with them.

SOURCES OF EXTERNAL RESOURCES

There are a variety of ways of finding the external resource appropriate for the organization and some of these are discussed below:

Vendors. Outside suppliers are in constant contact with others in the business, not necessarily just in their line of service. Thus, hardware vendors may know the name of a good maintenance technician, a scriptwriter may know the name of a good technical director, a graphic artist may know the name of a good director, and so on.

People in the business. Organization personnel can also be sources of potential external resources. One department member maybe in contact with certain external resources that may be appropriate for use by another. Other organizations, likewise, can be a valuable source of information on the location, availability and desirability of external resources. Head-hunters, professional organizations and institutions of learning can also provide leads.

Publications and trade shows. External resources very often advertise, are written up or publish articles in trade journals and publications. Some may also advertise their services in consumer publications. Both sources can be used as a means of finding the appropriate external resource. Trade shows are prime sources for learning about the suppliers who exhibit there and are happy to show their products. *Folio,* (New Canaan, CN) aimed at magazine and book publishing, is a good source of printers, for example, and *Video Expo* (Knowledge Industry Publications, Inc., White Plains, NY) is the best way to find out about video equipment and applications. Others include the Visual Communications Congress, NAVA (National Audio-Visual Association) and the NAB (National Association of Broadcasters).

FOOTNOTES

1. Some portions of this chapter are adapted, with permission, from Eugene Marlow, "Outside Suppliers," *Videography,* March 1978, Copyright United Business Publications, Inc.

10

The Evolving Media Center

What we define as the role and scope of the corporate media center of today may well change in the next decade. In an era of rapid social and technological change, media center managers must be aware of both emerging communications technologies and social trends, and how they will change the nature of the corporate media center. This chapter gives an overview of some of the new technologies and trends, and tries to judge just how the corporate media center will adjust to these changes.

TRENDS IN COMMUNICATIONS TECHNOLOGY

The Information Society

In the last decade several large companies in a major American industry have shown signs of decline. At first the problems did not seem related, but now the relationship is striking. What companies are they? You will remember them immediately: Penn-Central, Lockheed and the Chrysler Corporation; all companies related to the transportation industry.

Perhaps what we are experiencing is a change in the way we "transport" information. In a broad sense, we could say that the car, the train and the plane transport information physically. However, information can also be transported "electronically." What is emerging is a shift from an era of physical transportation of information to an era of electronic transportation. James Martin, in *The Wired Society*, supports this idea:

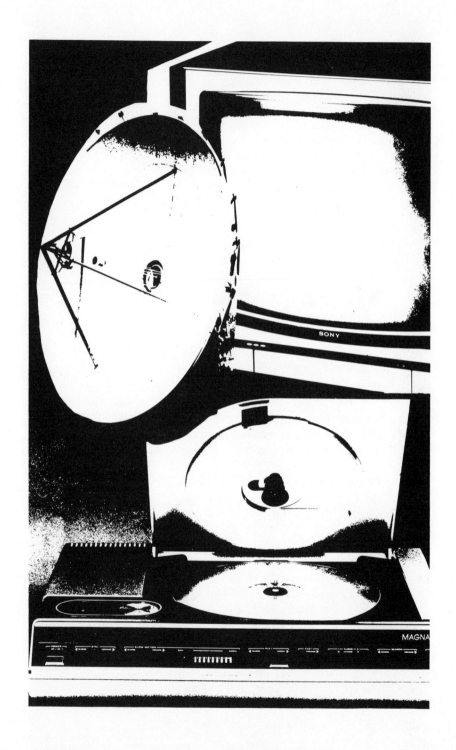

Telecommunications facilities can act as a substitute for much travel, with people able to see each other and operate machines at a great distance. They consume little energy from sunlight in space. New optical fiber cables, semi-conductor lasers that work with them, and microminature electronic circuitry are manufactured with silicon, one of the world earth's most abundant elements. Such satellites and fibers could transmit all the information the human race could possibly use.[1]

Martin also points to the potential of information retrieval facilities that give access to sports and financial information, weather forecasts, encyclopedias and vast stores of reports and documents. Citizens can watch their political representatives in action and register approval or protest. Telecommunications, he points out, will also allow people in small villages to work for large corporations.

In Martin's scenario multinational corporations are:

...Laced together with worldwide networks for telephones, instant mail and links between computers. Video conference rooms and computerized information systems increase the degree to which head-office executives guide corporate operations in other countries. Computers schedule fleets and optimize the use of resources on a worldwide basis. Money can be moved electronically from one country to another and switched to different currencies. There is worldwide management of capital, inventory control, product design, bulk purchasing, computer software, and so on. Local problem situations can trigger the instant attention of head-office staff.[2]

Martin further sees an expanded role for television working in tandem with the telephone system, an example of which is the viewdata system developed by the British Post Office. This system allows one to use the telephone to access computers which store information and programs, thus making vast quantities of information accessible to users when they want it.

Regarding the new telecommunications technologies, Martin observes that when they are used in conjunction with television channels, large quantities of information, and a greater variety of programming, can be delivered directly into the home.

Martin and other prominent experts foresee a wide range of uses for telecommunications in the home, among them: interactive television; telemedical services; still picture interaction, the use of home printers for electronic mail, message delivery, customized advertising; and finally, the use of home computer terminals for everything from domestic accounting to computer dating.[3]

Telecommunications will also provide a means for people to "talk back" to the sender — this possibility exists on a experimental level with the Qube system in Columbus, OH.

The Impact of Computers and Integrated Circuits

The futuristic scenario painted by Martin is in many ways a present reality. Nearly everyone today has a pocket calculator, and sales of home computers are increasing, as are the number of video games. The growth in the number and kind of electronic devices is due largely to the development of two interactive devices: the computer and integrated circuits. The first electronic computer, ENIAC (for Electronic Numerical Integrator and Calculator), was built in 1946. It consumed 140,000 watts of electricity and contained 18,000 vacuum tubes. In 1947 Bell Laboratories introduced the transistor, a tiny piece of semiconducting material, such as silicon or germanium. The transistor was the perfect mate for digital computers using a binary code. In 1959 Texas Instruments and Fairchild Semiconductor simultaneously announced the production of integrated circuits: single semiconductor chips containing several complete electronic circuits. By 1970 laboratories were producing chips with large scale integration of circuitry (LSI); thousands of integrated circuits crammed onto a single quarter inch of silicon.

Today, fully 100,000 transitors can be integrated on a chip. More computer power has been put into less and less space.[4] There are now, and have been for some time, electronic devices that create graphics, such as those manufactured by Intelligence System Corp., Tektronix, IBM and Hewlett-Packard. General Electric developed electronic graphic devices for simulation purposes for the National Aeronautics and Space Administration (NASA) space program. Such devices (called genigraphics) are now used for the generation of graphics and the ultimate transfer of these electronic images to 35mm slide format.

Integrated circuits have also helped spawn the home video market. The number of home video cassette recorders (VCRs) in Betamax and VHS formats is on the rise. *Madison Avenue* magazine, reports that most industry sources predict that home VCRs should be in 10% to 15% of TV-owning homes by 1985.[5]

Computer devices and integrated circuitry have invaded other aspects of the communications world, for example, with devices that program and run multimedia presentations. Computer-like devices also perform functions for video tape editing, color correction of film-to-tape transfers, and "timing" of film prints. All of these devices have computer-like mechanisms and integrated circuitry, as well as a keyboard terminal which allows the operator to manipulate the "information" in the device.

Cable Television

Other electronic technologies are affecting our personal and professional lives. Cable television, for example, distributes radio-frequency television signals to subscribers' TV sets via a coaxial cable and/ or optical fiber, rather than by broadcasting the signal over the airways. The cable, therefore, provides interference-free signals; moreover, whereas telephone lines are not presently able to carry the kind of video signals that coaxial or fiber optic cables can carry, the reverse is true. Cable television, born about 30 years ago out a need to bring television signals to communities that could not receive good broadcast signals, is becoming increasingly popular. The number of cable subscribers in the U.S. was 2.8 million in 1968 and a little over 19 million in 1979. Cable is projected to reach somewhere between 30 to 35 million subscribers by 1985.

Cable television is becoming more than just a means of transmitting a good television system. One company has installed a number of cable-energized burglary, fire and emergency alarm systems. Ralph M. Baruch, Chairman of the Board and Chief Executive Officer of Viacom International, also notes that the cable industry is experimenting with power distribution systems that could turn appliances on and off using a cable signal from a central computer.[6]

Cable technologies have also opened the way to interactive (two-way) television, such as the Qube system. Among the potential applications of interactive television are its use as an educational tool, in hospitals by doctors and patients (for therapy, patient education, etc.), for advertising and market research, and a variety of other functions.

One particularly significant use of interactive cable is information retrieval through a keyboard in the home. An example of such a system is videotext, or viewdata. The broadcast version of videotext is known as teletext, a term for systems that transmit alphanumeric data. With a properly modified television set (the viewer would have to equip the television set with a special decoder and keypad), a viewer can have continuous access to information, electronically.*

---

*For further information on videotext, the reader is referred to *Videotext: The Coming Revolution in Home/Office Information Retrieval*, Efrem Sigel, ed. (White Plains, NY: Knowledge Industry Publications, Inc., 1980).

Satellites

Satellite technology, together with the growth of cable systems, allows a programmer to direct electronic content at specific regions on demand. It creates the possiblity of a geometric increase in the number of programming possibilities.[7]

Satellite technology is creating the potential for the development of "electronic highways" heretofore not existent. Companies such as Satellite Business Systems (SBS) have been created for the sole purpose of business communications, such as voice communications, data processing, facsimile transmissions and two-way teleconferencing. However, as Gary Arlen, editor of *Satellite News* points out, satellites are not yet as widely used as cable systems, primarily because the number of satellites is limited as is their capacity. Since the demand for satellites is high, and will continue to increase, access is also expensive and likely to remain so for the next few years. However, the next generation of satellites (scheduled to go into orbit in the mid-1980s) will have a much greater capacity.[8]

Video Disc

The other major technology that has become a reality is the video disc. As John J. Reilly, President of DiscoVision, observed in early 1980, video disc technology represents "the merging of laser technology, computer technology and information storage technology."[9] He was, of course, not merely referring to the simple playback (or capacitance) video disc system, but to the interactive (laser optical) video disc that incorporates a microprocessor accessed by a hand-held device. This interactive capability allows the user to locate any frame on the video disc (or any part of the program) without time consuming searching. Some of the most significant aspects and major advantages of optical video disc technology are:

- The video disc resembles the long-playing record, except that it carries both images and sound. The video disc player is connected to a standard television set on which the image is viewed.
- The optical video disc has freeze-frame, slow motion and reverse capability, which makes it well-suited for educational and industrial applications.
- The video disc does not have to be duplicated in real time—a disc with two hours of programming can be duplicated in less than one minute.
- The optical video disc utilizes light from a laser for playback. Since there is no physical contact with the surface of the disc, it can be

used without wear. Furthermore, it has a protective coating so that dust, fingerprints or scratches have virtually no effect on picture quality.

• Each side of the disc can carry 54,000 frames or pictures, each of which can can be randomly accessed by a hand-held, programmable remote control unit. Thus an analog video disc containing the equivalent of 60 billion bits of data per disc side can be scanned in seconds.

• The optical video disc has two soundtracks which allow for stereophonic sound, or tracks in two different languages, or levels of instruction.[10, 11]

The interactive video disc could have a major impact on the way information is learned, since it combines several elements of instruction: printed text, audiovisual presentation, color and individualized instruction.*

Expanded data storage capabilities of the video disc are also on the rise. According to *Business Week*, the same video disc technology being developed for the consumer market will have a profound impact on the information processing business, as many computer equipment manufacturers "hope to piggyback on the high-volume consumer marketplace with a development of their own: optical disc products that use lasers not only to play back data, but also to engrave the data on the plastic disc."[13] Thus, the future for the video disc holds the promise of increased capacity for playback of information, as well as the possiblity of "writing" on the discs themselves.

THE CHANGING ENVIRONMENT

In conjunction with the new technological developments discussed above, there are certain trends in evidence which, in the decade of the 1980s and beyond, will influence corporate communications activities.

---

*Dr. Michael DeBloois, Director of the Center for Instructional Product Development at Utah State University, has developed a comparison between current instructional design model assumptions and probable new instructional design model assumptions as a result of the video disc. Among the significant changes that DeBloois' analysis reveals are: multi-dimensional development of materials and strategies, as opposed to linear; heterogeneous audience planning; multiple and continuing selection options for materials and formats, rather than one-time selection; integration of resource and presentation materials; and extended dissemination capacity.[12]

Demassification of Society

John Naisbitt, Senior Vice President of Yankelovich, Skelly and White, notes certain trends which he feels point to a "demassification" of society—trends that will have an impact on the organizational environment in which the media center operates, notably:

- The United States is rapidly shifting from a mass industrial society to an information society.
- There is more decentralization than centralization taking place in America.
- There are the beginnings of a job revolution in America, a basic restructuring of the work environment from top-down to bottom-up.

Essentially, these trends are indicative of changes in the pattern and flow of communication, and as such will have a direct impact on not only the media center's corporate environment, but on its operations as well.

Employee Motivation

David Rockefeller, when Chairman of the Chase Manhattan Bank, observed that the increasing numbers of college and business school graduates will soon swell the ranks of middle and upper management, leaving many individuals unable to find positions commensurate with their training—a situation already in evidence today. Motivating these employees, he feels, will pose a "supreme test" for the manager of the future. [15]

In addition, Alvin Toffler describes the workers of the Third Wave, the "new workers:"

> Workers are forced to cope with more frequent changes in their tasks and with a blinding succession of personnel transfers, product changes and reorganizations.
>
> What Third Wave employers increasingly need, therefore, are men and women who accept responsibility, who understand how their work dovetails with others', who can handle ever larger tasks, who adapt swiftly to changed circumstances and are sensitively tuned in to the people around them. [16]

Media center employees and managers, who are so much a part of communications advances, will be in the vanguard of the Third Wave.

IMPLICATIONS FOR THE FUTURE

The developments reviewed in the preceeding pages lead to certain general conclusions, and possible implications, for the future.

(1) There is a trend away from homogeneity and toward heterogeneity. Programming for, and marketing to, mass audiences may give way to regional and even local programming; "narrowcasting" is a concept already much in evidence. Cable systems and satellites will help foster this trend. This may result in regional or local marketing or public relations programming being produced by some media centers directly. In addition, the impact of burgeoning cable systems, together with satellites, augurs a change in the function of existing broadcasting systems as we know them. The new electronic highways will enable programmers to bypass the usual distribution systems.

(2) External communications activities will change in the next decade. The focus on local or regional politics will cause organizations to modify their government relations activities.

(3) Internal communications activities will also change in the next 10 years. More and more workers will be employed in information processing activities, as opposed to "manufacturing" activities. There will be better educated employees, including more women and minorities, striving for higher levels of achievement. This will cause stresses in many organizations which will, in turn, change the configuration of internal organizational communications systems: they may have to become more personal and frequent because employees will require more contact with higher management, as well as more independent decision-making opportunities.

(4) Electronic technology will continue to march forward, with more and more electronics merging into more and more devices that previously may not have been touched by it. Increasing numbers of electronic devices are interactive, and this trend will continue. Furthermore, the information storage capacity of such devices is on the rise, particularly with respect to the computer and the video disc.

(5) Electronic devices will become less expensive for the recording, manipulation, editing and retrieval of information, while the more traditional information carrying devices, such as paper and film, will be used less as a news or even entertainment medium. The decrease in the use of film for news programming and the increase in the use of ENG-type video cameras and recording equipment is but one example of the probable demise of film as a dominant communications technology.

(6) As the cost for disseminating information electronically decreases, and its efficiency as a communications medium increases, there will be a decrease in the use of paper as a mass communications device. Increased costs of mailing and of producing paper, and the unwieldiness of information in print form as compared to its electronic equivalent, will contribute to this decline. However, this does not necessarily mean the complete abandonment of paper as an information-bearing technology. On the contrary, paper will have other functions; for example, as the hardcopy form of information retrieved electronically.

(7) The growth of electronic devices in the home, in particular home video cassette recorders, video discs and viewdata, could well usher in an era in which organizations produce programming that will be viewed by employees in the home, rather than just at work.

(8) Organizational use of electronic devices will increase as the need for higher employee productivity increases. The increased use of electronic devices for word processing and data processing is but one example.

(9) More manufacturing operations will be handled by machines run by computers. As a result, a lower percentage of workers will be engaged in manufacturing work as machines do more manual labor. This trend should continue for at least two decades.

IMPLICATIONS FOR THE MEDIA CENTER

These fundamental changes in the larger societal and technological landscape will have a direct impact on various aspects of the media center, as discussed below.

Media Product

The output of organizational media centers will probably increase as the pace of change and the pressures of internal and external communications activities increase. Technological changes, especially in administrative, manufacturing and communications systems, will create the need for informational and training programs. For example, as more and more organizations switch over to electronic word processing, training programs will have to be created to train both users and administrators. As increasing numbers of organizations use machines to direct manufacturing operations, the need for programming to inform and train personnel on the use, operation and maintenance of these machines will become greater. As more organizations use more sophisticated electronic systems for communications, the need for information and training programs on these systems will increase. Furthermore, the process will be self-generating as newer and more capable electronic systems are brought into use.

The advent of electronic devices will intensify the need for increased communications activities among various components of the organization. This will be especially true of the larger, far-flung multinational organizations. While this does not mean a tendency towards centralization from a communications or control point of view, it does mean that in a changing external environment, organizations will require increased communications to maintain equilibrium. The need to create understanding among the various organizational components will become imperative to organizational survival. This will again translate into an increased need for communications product.

The need for more communications activity together with the rising cost of travel will cause greater organizational use of teleconferencing systems. Together with the increased use of satellites for such purposes, teleconferencing will probably reduce business travel significantly.

The development of cable systems in all their various configurations, fostered by the increased use of satellites, could have an impact on the marketing and advertising of organizational products. This in turn will influence the nature, form and origination of marketing and advertising programming. It is conceivable that via a combination of cable systems, organizations will develop regional and even local marketing and advertising programming. This type of audience segmentation may result in more professional in-house media centers becoming involved in the development, production and distribution of such programming.

Marketing information directed at organizational salesforces should also increase as competition, both domestic and foreign, intensifies in the 1980s. Management communications programming will also intensify as central management must communicate more frequently with field managers.

It is well to note that this general increase in the use of media center capabilities, as a result of the increased need for communications, will also increase the use of external resources.

Hardware Systems

Organizational media centers will experience inevitable changes in hardware systems in the 1980s. As electronics continues to pervade the culture, we should see, for example, the further development and use of computer-like devices for the creation of graphics. Similar devices will be used for the creation and manufacture of 35mm slides. Moreover, it is possible that the need for hardcopy graphics in the form of 35mm slides will decrease as other kinds of computer-like devices become accessible to managers, so that data, statistics and trends can be created electronically, even up to the last minute before a presentation.

Video cameras will contain more electronic control devices; even tubes may disappear. Cameras will become smaller, more sophisticated, more capable and cheaper. Devices for electronic editing will become more flexible, sophisticated and less expensive. Video disc technology may move toward the development of devices that both playback and record video information. If this happens on a level that can be afforded by most, it is conceivable that video tape may drop out as a communications technology, just as it appears that film will. Moveover, the further development of large screen video projection may answer the need for large audience viewing of programs originated and produced on video tape or video disc.

Thus, by the next decade, organizations may no longer be weighing the relative merits of filmstrips versus film or video tape, but rather weighing merits of video disc versus video tape — filmstrips, slide/tape, Super 8mm, and 16mm film distribution having vanished almost altogether.

Organizations will also face the possibility of installing teleconferencing facilities and satellite up/down links as communications via these technologies increase in frequency. By the end of the decade, teleconferencing may be as casual a communications activity among organizational management as picking up the telephone to make a trans-continental phone call is today.

Organizational Changes

There will also be a converging of technologies from other parts of the organization. The first and most obvious convergence should be with regard to teleconferencing. Organizational media center operations will "bump" into hardware systems operated by the telecommunications department, who, in turn, will be bumping into technologies operated by the electronic data processing department. Administrative operations, such as word processing and electronic mail, may also converge. The reason for this increased interaction among seemingly disparate organizational departments is that teleconferencing technologies, particularly via satellite communications, can handle all the various communications activities: voice communications, data processing, facsimile transmission and two-way, wide-band video communications.

In Chapter 3, an "ideal" model for the organization of the media center was presented. While some organizations more or less reflect this kind of model, as of this writing the model does not represent the vast majority. This should change in the 1980s. The tendency toward centralization of media center activities will come as a result of two trends: an organizational focus on increased productivity, and the increased use of electronic technologies.

As organizations move towards maximizing resources in a world of limited resources, they will look for ways to make the best use out of existing resources. This may mean bringing seemingly disparate activities together and managing these resources under one organizational umbrella. Furthermore, as more electronic devices are used in media center activities, we should see a continued shift away from the manual creation of communications products, such as graphic arts and photography, to the electronic creation of such products. Thus, by the end of the 1980s media production activities, whether graphic, photographic or electronic, will have electronic/computer technologies in common. In turn, it should become obvious that these activities belong together.

As media center activities become more electronic and computerized, it is conceivable that these activities will have more in common with telecommunications, data processing, and word processing as opposed to marketing, training or corporate communications. It is possible, therefore, that the media center will move away, organizationally, from its traditional home, and toward a new area with which the media center will have more in common—technology.

On a broader scale, the organizational need to better use communications systems and better control overall organizational communications activities may result in the centralizing of other communications functions. It is possible that by the next decade, more organizations will have merged their training, employee communications, advertising and marketing, press relations, government relations, community relations, media center, and other "communications systems," such as telecommunications, into one "macro" communications activity. Such an activity might be divided into three major areas:

- Internal communications: training, employee communications.
- External communications: advertising/marketing, press relations, government relations, community relations, investor relations.
- Media center operations: graphic arts, film, video tape, video disc, teleconferencing, telecommunications, word processing, data processing.

In this context, both internal and external communications activities are "audience" oriented, whereas the media center operation is software and hardware oriented. Media center staffs would have the overall function of translating communications content into a media form (software) and using various technologies (hardware) to deliver that content to the appropriate audience.

Implications for the Media Center Staff

In the 1980s the type of expertise found among the media center staff will change. The further development of video tape technologies (cameras, recorders and editing equipment) will necessitate a great deal of upgrading of the skills of technicians and producer/directors. While manufacturer advertisements give the impression that the newer video tape technologies make production and post-production a lot more accessible, it must be remembered that maintenance becomes more complex. Thus, organizations can expect an increase in the number of personnel involved in media center activities, especially in the technical area. Moreover, existing and future personnel will be expected to have a higher degree of understanding of the communications problem-solving process, existing and developing technologies, and organizational practices.

The video disc, especially, will change the nature of media center staff expertise. Whereas programming for slide, film and video tape is linear in presentation, programming for the video disc is not. Moreover, video disc programming will present opportunities for the use of still graphics, as well as motion graphics (such as film and video tape). When to use what medium for informational or instructional purposes will become of paramount importance in the effectiveness of video disc programming. As the use of video disc increases, media center employees (especially producer/directors) should find themselves in much greater contact with training personnel who, presumably, are the experts in instructional design. The video disc, because of its high interactive capability, will do more than any other technology to bring together media center and training department staffs. This should foster even greater cooperation among the two professional groups, which will have a net positive effect on the organization.

All personnel in the media center will be affected by the electronic technologies. Graphic artists may find themselves designing and executing graphics at an electronic keyboard rather than at a drawing table, using a television-like screen to make changes in design, colors and hue, both for pictorial representations and word copy. Computer-graphics devices may have a substantial impact on the sale of drawing implements.

Photographers, too, may be affected by the advent of electronic technology. The creation of 35mm slides has already been affected by the development of electronic devices that create graphics electronically and then convert them to either 35mm slide or paper hardcopy. Motion film (Super 8mm and 16mm) may very well see its demise in the 1980s, as video tape and video disc recording devices are used more. Writers, too, may find themselves working at word processing terminals, rather than typewriters.

A FINAL WORD

While it appears that many corporate media centers will experience an evolutionary transformation during the 1980s, not all media centers will. Moreover, it is not necessarily true that with the advent of such technologies as computer graphics, teleconferencing and video disc, suddenly all organizational media centers will become gorged with sophisticated electronic gadgetry and find themselves staffed with electronic media production superstars.

On the contrary, the above scenario may be limited to those media centers with sufficient need and means for such hardware, software and personnel. Yet, many organizations—perhaps all—will be touched by the evolution of electronic technologies. Moreover, new technologies will not completely obsolesce existing technologies. The history of technology teaches us that newer technologies have the affect of changing the function of existing technologies, rather than making them obsolete altogether. For example, while speech was once the primary form of communications, writing and print have not, obviously, done away with it. Photographic and electronic media have not done away with writing and print. Looking to the future, highly interactive communications media, such as teleconferencing and the video disc, should not do away with photography and video tape technologies altogether, but will probably change their functions.

For example, video tape could change the long-term function of print as an organizational mass communications tool. The quintessential example of the impact of video tape on print exists at Sikorsky Aircraft (CT). In the last few years Sikorsky has gone through a transformation of its workforce and output. As a result, management revamped its employee communications programs. One phase of its new employee communications program was the development of a daily employee news show on video, which transformed the print house organ from a news medium to a feature medium.

Film, too, may see a change. Whereas film was once relied upon heavily as a news medium by the broadcast networks and local stations, it has been largely replaced by video tape and electronic news gathering hardware. However, film continues to be used as an entertainment medium; e.g., for the movies shown in theaters, and on home television systems (either broadcast, pay cable, video cassette or video disc). However, we should note that more and more movies are being shot on video tape and transferred to the film medium for distribution and presentation, so that film's survival as a production medium may be in question.

The function of video tape may also change in the next decade, especially if video discs are developed (at a cheap enough price) that play back *and* record video information. If this occurs—and the technologies are in the process of development now—it could very well change the function of video tape as a communications medium both in consumer markets and organizational life.

Further, while new technologies will continue to appear, this does not mean to say people will readily accept them. In the organizational context, at least, employees tend to resist technological change. It is entirely possible, for example, that middle managers will resist the use of video teleconferencing because it will mean "not getting away from the office." If, indeed, teleconferencing cuts down on business travel, this could be perceived as a loss of status and prestige. Another example is the resistance of managers to the use of keyboard terminals to access information banks, which may be perceived as a technician's function.

Be that as it may, new technologies, especially if they are more effective and efficient than existing technologies, have an historical habit of taking hold anyway. It is not really a matter of "if" new technologies will have a meaningful impact, but "when."

The 1980s will witness change, both socially and technologically. Organizational and media center management must be prepared for it. Presumably, change is the primary reason for the media center: change creates the need to communicate. Media center staffs prepared both technically and attitudinally for change will benefit the most.

The 1980s will present many problems for organizations; but this will also serve as an opportunity for media centers to help organizations through an era that will witness the transformation of our civilization from a "resource processing" (manufacturing) to an "information processing" society.

FOOTNOTES

1. Martin, James, *The Wired Society* (Englewood, Cliffs, NJ: Prentice-Hall, 1978).

2. *Ibid*, p. 13.

3. *Ibid*, pp. 154-157.

4. Background information for this section is from "Machines That Think," *Newsweek,* June 30, 1980.

5. *Madison Avenue*, June 1980.

6. Baruch, Ralph M., "Lifestyle Revolution in the Television Age." Speech given before the Town Hall of California, Los Angeles, December 4, 1979.

7. Goldman, Andrew, "The Role of Cable TV and the Changing Technology: The Importance of Being Different." Speech given before the ANA Television Workshop, New York, March 4, 1980.

8. Personal interview with Gary Arlen, summer 1980.

9. Speech by John J. Reilly. Given before the American Video Institute, Columbia University, NY, 1980.

10. Roberts, Martin, "Video Disc Capabilities and Effects." Remarks given at the Hearing of the House of Representatives, Government Activities and Transportation Subcommittee of the Committee on Government Operations, Federal Building, Los Angeles, CA, 1979.

11. Sigel, Efrem, et al., *Video Discs: The Technology, the Applications and the Future* (White Plains, NY: Knowledge Industry Publications, Inc. 1980).

12. DeBloois, Michael, "Exploring New Design Models," *Educational Industrial Television,* May 1979.

13. *Business Week,* July 7, 1980.

14. Naisbitt, John, "What's Really Happening in the U.S." Speech given before the Foresight Group, Stockholm, Sweden, September 20, 1979.

15. Speech by David Rockefeller. Given before the Commonwealth Club of San Francisco, November 2, 1979.

16. Toffler, Alvin, *The Third Wave* (New York: William Morrow & Co., 1980).

Introduction to Appendixes

There are five appendixes in this section.

Appendix I is a bibliography of over 400 books in nine major areas: Business Communications; General Communications; Engineering & Technical Functions; Graphic Arts/Print Production; General Management; Media Management; Public Relations; Training and Development; and Video/Film/Multimedia Production. General Management has been further sub-divided into the following categories: budgeting, managerial dynamics, human resource management, analytical tools, financial management, decision/management and leadership. This bibliography is an excellent reference for anyone who would like to gain a reading knowledge of what is required to manage a corporate media center.

Appendix II is a listing of the major organizations and associations involved in various aspects of communications, such as: management, engineering and technical subjects, writing, film processing, graphic arts, multimedia production, film production, film animation, still photography, training, video tape production and public relations.

Appendix III is a listing of major trade and professional publications in the various communications areas mentioned.

Appendix IV lists the major colleges and universities that provide courses of instruction in media production, such as: photography, graphic arts, film, video tape and multimedia production.

Appendix V is a listing of the major competitions in the areas of graphic arts, still photography, slide photography, film production, multimedia production and video tape production.

Appendix I: Suggested Readings

BUSINESS COMMUNICATIONS

Barbara, Dominick A., *How to Make People Listen To You.* Springfield, IL: Charles C. Thomas Publishers, 1971.

Gieselman, R.D., ed., *Readings in Business Communication.* 2nd ed. Champaign IL: Stipes Publishing Co., 1978.

Haney, William V., *Communication and Interpersonal Relations.* 4th ed. Homewood, IL: Richard D. Irwin, 1979.

Houp, Kenneth W. and Thomas E. Pearsall, *Reporting Technical Information.* 3rd ed. Beverly Hills, CA: Glencoe Press, 1977.

Lesikar, Raymond V., *Report Writing for Business.* 5th ed. Homewood, IL: Richard D. Irwin, 1977.

Menning, J.M., C.W. Wilkinson and P.B. Clarke, *Communication Through Letters and Reports.* 6th ed. Homewood, IL: Richard D. Irwin, 1976.

Strunk, William, Jr. and E.B. White, *The Elements of Style.* 3rd ed. New York: Macmillan, 1979.

Weeks, Francis W. and Daphne Jameson, *Principles of Business Communication.* 2nd ed. Champaign, IL: Stipes Publishing Co., 1979.

GENERAL COMMUNICATIONS

Barnouw, Eric, *Mass Communication.* New York: Holt, Rinehart & Winston, 1958.

Becker, Stephen, *Comic Art in America: A Social History of the Funnies.* New York: Simon and Schuster, 1960.

Berelson, Bernard, *Content Analysis in Communications Research.* New York: Free Press, 1952.

Berelson, Bernard and Norris Janowitz, eds., *Public Opinion and Communication.* New York: Free Press, 1953.

Duncan, Hugh D., *Communication and the Social Order.* New York: Oxford University Press, 1962.

Ellul, Jacques, *The Technological Society.* New York: Vintage, 1967.

Portions of this bibliography have been excerpted from the publications of the American Business Communication Association, American Management Association, American Society for Training & Development, Inc. (May 1980 *Training and Development Journal),* Public Relations Society of America and the New York University Media Ecology Dept. Used with permission.

Fromm, Erich, *The Sane Society*. New York: Holt, Rinehart & Winston, 1955.

Fuller, R. Buckminster, *Ideas and Integrities*. New York: Collier, 1969.

Fuller, R. Buckminster, *Utopia or Oblivion: The Prospects for Humanity*. New York: Bantam Books, 1969.

Hogben, Lancelot, *From Cave Painting to Comic Strips: A Kaleidoscope of Human Communication*. New York: Chanticleer Press, 1949.

Katz, Daniel, et al., *Public Opinion and Propoganda*. Hinsdale, IL: Dryden Press, 1954.

Klapper, Joseph T., *The Effects of Mass Communication*. New York: Free Press, 1960.

Knight, Arthur, *The Liveliest Art: A Panoramic History of the Movies*. New York: Mentor Books, 1959.

Lowenthal, Leo, *Literature, Popular Culture and Society*. New York: Spectrum, 1961.

McLuhan, Marshall, *The Gutenberg Galaxy: The Making of Typographic Man*. New York: Signet, 1969.

McLuhan, Marshall, *The Mechanical Bride: Folklore of Industrial Man*. Boston, MA: Beacon Press, 1967.

McLuhan, Marshall, *Understanding Media: The Extension of Man*. New York: McGraw-Hill, 1965.

McLuhan, Marshall and Quentin Fiore, *War and Peace in the Global Village*. New York: Bantam Books, 1968.

MacGowan, Kenneth, *Behind the Screen: The History and Techniques of the Motion Picture* New York: Delta Books, 1960.

Matson, Floyd and Ashley Montague, eds., *The Human Dialogue: Perspectives on Communication*. New York: Free Press, 1967.

Mott, Frank Luther, *Golden Multitudes: The Story of Best Sellers in the United States*. New York: Macmillan, 1947.

Mumford, Lewis, *The Myth of the Machine: Techniques and Human Development*. New York: Harcourt Brace Jovanovich, 1957.

Osgood, Charles et al., *The Measurement of Meaning*. Urbana, IL: University of Illinois Press, 1957.

Peterson, Theodore, *Magazines in the Twentieth Century*. Urbana, IL: University of Illinois Press, 1957.

Pool, Ithiel de Sola, ed., *Trends in Content Analysis*. Urbana, IL: University of Illinois Press, 1959.

Rokeach, Milton, *The Open and Closed Mind: Investigation in the Nature of Belief Systems and Personality Systems*. New York: Basic Books, 1960.

Schramm, Wilbur, ed., *Mass Communications*. Urbana, IL: University of Illinois Press, 1960.

Shannon, Claude and Warren Weaver, *The Mathematical Theory of Communication.* Urbana, IL: University of Illinois Press, 1949.

Skornia, Harry J., *Television and Society: An Inquest and Agenda for Improvement.* New York: McGraw-Hill, 1965.

Toffler, Alvin, *Future Shock.* New York: Random House, 1970.

Van Laau, Thomas F. and Robert B. Lyons, *Language and the Newsstand: A Critical Reader.* New York: Charles Scribner's Sons, 1968.

Warshow, Robert, *The Immediate Experience: Movies, Comics, Theatre and Other Aspects of Popular Culture.* Garden City, NY: Doubleday, 1964.

Weiner, Norbert, *The Human Use of Human Beings: Cybernetics and Society.* Garden City, NY: Doubleday, 1956.

ENGINEERING & TECHNICAL FUNCTIONS

Berliner, Oliver, *Color TV Studio Design and Operation: For CATV, School and Industry.* Blue Ridge Summit, PA: Tab Books, 1975.

Bermingham, Alan, et al., The Small TV Studio. New York: Hastings House, 1975.

Brown, James W., *Educational Media Yearbook.* New York: R.R. Bowker (annual publication).

Campbell, Goy, et al., *Radio and TV Servicing — Intermediate Course.* ERIC Clearinghouse: ED 139 936.

Crowhurst, Norman H., *Audio Systems Handbook.* Blue Ridge Summit, PA: Tab Books, 1969.

Daynes, Rodney, *Videodisc Technology Use Through 1986: A Delphi Study.* ERIC Clearinghouse: ED 145 823.

Diamant, Lincoln, ed., *The Broadcast Communications Dictionary.* New York: Hastings House, 1978.

Eastman Kodak Co., *Preservation of Photographs.* Rochester, NY: Kodak Publication F-30, 1979.

Eastman Kodak Co., *Versatility in Reprographics.* Rochester, NY: Kodak Publications, Dept. 454., 343 State St., Rochester, NY 14650.

Ennes, Harold, *Television Broadcasting: Equipment, Systems, and Operating Fundamentals.* New York: Howard W. Sams & Co., 1971.

Frater, Charles B., *Sound Recording for Motion Pictures.* Cranbury, NJ: A.S. Barnes, 1979.

Hansen, G.L., *Introduction to Solid State Television Systems.* Englewood Cliffs, NJ: Prentice Hall, 1969.

Herickes, Sally, *The Audio-Visual Equipment Directory.* Fairfax, VA: National Audio-Visual Association, 1979.

Jorgenson, Finn, *Handbook of Magnetic Recording.* Blue Ridge Summit, PA: Tab Books, 1970.

Kennedy, M. Carlos, ed., *Digital Video — Volume 2.* Scarsdale, NY: Society of Motion Picture and Television Engineers, 1979.

McGinty, Gerald P., *Videocassette Recorders: Theory and Servicing.* New York: Gregg/McGraw-Hill, 1979.

Nisbett, Alec, *The Technique of the Sound Studio - Radio and Recording.* New York: Hastings House, 1965.

Nisbett, Alec, *The Use of Microphones.* New York: Hastings House, 1974.

Oringle, Robert S., *Audio Control Handbook.* 4th ed. New York: Hastings House, 1972.

Pula, Fred J., *Application and Operation of Audio-Visual Equipment in Education.* New York: John Wiley & Sons, 1968.

Robinson, J.F., *Videotape Recording: Theory and Practice.* New York: Hastings House, 1975.

Ross, Rodger J., *Color Film for Color Television.* New York: Hastings House, 1970.

Showalter, Leonard C., *Closed-Circuit TV for Engineers and Technicians.* Indianapolis, IN: Bobbs-Merrill Co., 1969.

Sigel, Efrem, et al., *Video Discs: The Technology, the Applications and the Future.* White Plains, NY: Knowledge Industry Publications, Inc., 1980.

Sigel, Efrem with Colin McIntyre, Max Wilkinson and Joe Roizen, *Videotext: The Coming Revolution in Home/Office Information Retrieval.* White Plains, NY: Knowledge Industry Publications, Inc., 1980.

White, Gordon, *Video Recording.* New York: Crane, Russak, 1972.

GRAPHIC ARTS/PRINT PRODUCTION

Albarn, Keith, et al., *The Language of Pattern: An Enquiry Inspired by Islamic Decoration.* New York: Harper & Row, 1974.

Cardamone, Tom, *Advertising Agency and Studio Skills: A Guide to the Preparation of Art & Mechanicals for Reproduction.* Cincinnati, OH: Watson-Guptill Publications, 1970.

Carter, David E., ed., *Corporate Identity Manuals.* New York: Art Direction Book Co., 1978.

Carter, David E., ed., *Designing Corporate Symbols.* New York: Art Direction Book Co., 1975.

The Colorpedia. New York: Random House, Inc. (Includes an 820 page Alphapedia; a 48 page Time Chart; and an 80 page Atlas).

Craig, James, *Designing with Type*. Cincinnati, OH: Watson-Guptill Publications, 1971.

Croy, Peter, *Graphic Design and Reproduction Techniques*. New York: Hastings House, 1972.

Firpo, Patrick, Lester Alexander, Cludia Katayanagi and Steve Ditlea, *Copyart: The First Complete Guide to the Copy Machine*. New York: Richard Marek Publishers, 1978.

Goodchild, Jon and Bill Henkin, *By Design: A Graphics Sourcebook of Materials, Equipment and Services*. New York: Quick Fox, 1980.

Gorb, Peter, ed., *Living By Design*. Cincinnati, OH: Watson-Guptill Publications, 1978.

Graham, Walter, *Complete Guide to Paste-Up*. Philadelphia, PA: North American Publishing Co., 1975.

Halas, John, ed., *Computer Animation,* New York: Hastings House, 1974.

Hurtburt, Allen, *Layout*. Cincinnati, OH: Watson-Guptill Publications, 1977.

Kleper, Michael L., *Understanding Phototypesetting*. Philadelphia, PA: North American Publishing Co., 1976.

Lem, Dean Phillip, *The New Graphics Master*. New York: Art Direction Book Co., 1977.

Maier, Manfred, *Basic Principles of Design*. 4 volumes. New York: Van Nostrand Reinhold, 1978.

A Manual of Style, Chicago, IL: University of Chicago Press, 1979.

The Picture Reference File — a Compendium. Vol.1. New York: Hart Publishing Company, 1976.

Rasberry, Leslie, *Computer Age Copyfitting*. New York: Art Direction Book Co., 1978.

Ruder, Emil, *Typography: A Manual of Design*. New York: Hastings House, 1967.

Ruegg, Ruedi and Godi Frohlich, *Basic Typography: Handbook of Technique and Design*. New York: Hastings House, 1972.

Stevenson, George A., *The Graphic Arts Encyclopedia*. New York: McGraw-Hill, 1968.

Vicary, Richard, *Manual of Advanced Lithography*. New York: Charles Scribner's Sons, 1977.

Waldman, Stu and Marty Goldstein, eds., *The Creative Black Book*. New York: Friendly Publications, Inc., 1979.

GENERAL MANAGEMENT

Budgeting

Cheek, Logan M., *Zero-Based Budgeting Comes of Age.* New York: American Management Associations, 1977.

Ewing, David W., *The Practice of Planning.* New York: Harper & Row, 1968.

Matthews, Lawrence M., *Practical Operating Budgeting.* New York: McGraw-Hill, 1977.

Nemmers, Erwin E., *Managerial Economics: Text and Cases.* New York: McGraw-Hill, 1962.

Pyhrr, Peter A., *Zero-Based Budgeting.* New York: John Wiley & Sons, 1973.

Rachlin, Robert, *Return-on-Investment — Strategies for Profit.* Marr Publications, 1976.

Rautenstrauch, Walter and Raymond Villers, *Budgetary Control.* Scranton, PA: Funk & Wagnalls, 1968.

Sweeney, Allen and John N. Wisner, Jr., *Budgeting Fundamentals for Nonfinancial Executives.* New York: American Managment Associations, 1975.

Managerial Dynamics

Dale, Ernest, *Management: Theory and Practice.* New York: McGraw-Hill, 1973.

Davis, Ralph, *The Fundamentals of Top Management.* New York: Harper & Row, 1951.

Dowling, William, ed., *Effective Management & the Behavioral Sciences: Conversations from Organizational Dynamics.* New York: American Management Associations, 1978.

Drucker, Peter, *Management: Tasks, Responsibilites, Practices.* New York: Harper & Row, 1974.

Drucker, Peter F., *The Practice of Management.* New York: Harper & Row, 1954.

Ewing, David W., ed., *Long-Range Planning for Management.* New York: Harper & Row, 1972.

Famularo, Joseph J., *Organization Planning Manual.* New York: American Management Associations, 1979.

Hampton, David R., et al., *Organizational Behavior and the Practice of Management.* New York: Scott, Foresman, 1978.

Hargreaves, John and Jan Dauman, *Business Survival and Social Change.* New York: John Wiley & Sons, 1975.

Herzberg, Frederick, *The Managerial Choice: To Be Efficient and To Be Human.* New York: Dow-Jones/Irwin, 1976.

Heyel, Carl, ed., *The Encyclopedia of Management.* New York: Van Nostrand Reinhold, 1973.

Koontz, Harold, *Appraising Managers as Managers.* New York:McGraw-Hill, 1971.

Koontz, Harold, and Cyril O'Donnell, *Principles of Management.* New York: McGraw-Hill, 1972.

Lindberg, Roy A., *The Foundations of Management.* Dobbs Ferry, NY: Oceana Publications, 1973.

Litterer, Joseph A., *The Analysis of Organizations.* New York: John Wiley & Sons, 1973.

Mali, Paul, *Managing by Objectives.* New York: John Wiley & Sons, 1972.

McGregor, Douglas, Warren G. Bennis and Caroline McGregor, eds., *The Professional Manager.* New York: McGraw-Hill, 1967.

Moore, Russell, ed., *AMA Management Handbook.* New York: American Management Associations, 1970.

Mott, Paul E., *The Characteristics of Effective Organizations.* New York: Harper & Row, 1972.

Newman, William H., et al., *The Process of Management.* Englewood Cliffs, NJ: Prentice-Hall, 1977.

Rothschild, William E., *Putting It All Together: A Guide to Strategic Thinking.* New York: American Management Associations, 1976.

Skibbins, Gerald J., *Organizational Evolution: A Program for Managing Radical Change.* New York: American Management Associations, 1974.

Human Resource Management

Bogard, Morris R., *The Manager's Stylebook: Communication Skills to Improve your Performance.* Englewood Cliffs, NJ: Prentice-Hall, 1979.

Buskirk, Richard H., *Handbook of Managerial Tactics.* Boston, MA: Cahners Books International, 1976.

Dinsmore, Francis W., *Developing Tomorrow's Managers Today.* New York: American Management Associations, 1975.

Doctoroff, Michael, *Synergistic Management: Creating the Climate for Superior Performance.* New York: American Management Associations, 1978.

Drake, John D., *Interviewing for Managers.* New York: American Management Associations, 1972.

Flory, Charles D., ed., *Managers for Tomorrow.* New York: New American Library, 1971.

Golightly, Henry O., *Managing With Style: And Making It Work for You.* New York: American Management Associations, 1977.

Humble, John, *Improving the Performance of the Experienced Manager.* New York: McGraw-Hill, 1974.

Johnson, Robert G., *The Appraisal Interview Guide.* New York: American Management Associations, 1979.

Keefe, Wiliam F., *Open Minds: The Forgotten Side of Communication.* New York: American Management Associations, 1975.

Kellogg, Marion S., *What to Do About: Performance Appraisal.* New York: American Management Associations, 1975.

Koontz, Harold, *Appraising Managers as Managers.* New York: McGraw-Hill, 1971.

Lazarus, Sy., *Loud and Clear: A Guide to Effective Communication.* New York: American Management Associations, 1975.

Lefton, Robert E., et al., *Effective Motivation Through Performance Appraisal.* New York: John Wiley & Sons, 1977.

Lesly, Philip, *How We Discommunicate.* New York: American Management Associations, 1979.

McFarland, Dalton E., *Action Strategies for Managerial Achievement.* New York: American Management Associations, 1977.

McMurry, Robert N., *The Maverick Executive.* New York: American Management Associations, 1974.

Morrisey, George L., *Appraisal and Development Through Objectives and Results.* Reading, MA: Addison-Wesley, 1972.

People and Performance: The Best of Peter Drucker. New York: Harper & Row, 1977.

Potter, B.A., *Turning Around: The Behavioral Approach to Managing People.* New York: American Management Associations, 1980.

Sanzotta, Donald, *Motivational Theories and Applications for Managers.* New York: American Management Associations, 1977.

Silber, Mark B. and V. Clayton Sherman, *Managerial Performance and Promotability.* New York: American Management Associations, 1974.

Smith, Howard P. and Paul J. Brouwer, *Performance Appraisal and Human Development.* Reading, MA: Addison-Wesley, 1977.

Tannehill, Robert E., *Motivation and Management Development.* New York: Petrocelli Books, 1972.

Tracey, William R., *Managing Training and Development Systems.* New York: American Management Associations, 1974.

Williams, M. R., *Performance Appraisal in Management.* New York: Crane, Russak, 1972.

Wortman, Max S., Jr. and JoAnn Sperling, *Defining the Manager's Job.* New York: American Management Associations, 1975.

Yuill, Bruce and Dan Steinhoff, *Developing Managers in Organizations.* New York: John Wiley & Sons, 1975.

Analytical Tools of Management

Ackoff, Russell L., *A Concept of Corporate Planning.* New York: John Wiley & Sons, 1970.

Argenti, John, *Systematic Corporate planning,* New York: Halstead Press, 1977.

Ewing, David W., ed., *Long-Range Planning for Management.* New York: Harper & Row, 1972.

Green, Edward J., *Workbook for Corporate Planning.* New York: American Managemnt Associations, 1970.

Hussey, David., *Corporate Planning: Theory and Practice.* Elmsford, NY: Pergamon Press, 1974.

Hussey, David., *Introducing Corporate Planning.* Elmsford, NY: Pergamon Press, 1976.

Kastens, Merritt L., *Long-Range Planning for Your Business: An Operating Manual.* New York: American Management Associations, 1976.

King, William, R. and David I. Cleland, *Strategic Planning and Policy.* New York: Van Nostrand Reinhold, 1978.

Steiner, George A., *Strategic Planning: What Every Manager MUST Know.* New York: Free Press, 1979.

Financial Management

Archer, Stephen H. and Charles A. D'Ambrosio, *Business Finance: Theory and Management.* New York: Macmillan, 1972.

Dauten, Carl A. and Merle T. Welshans, *Principles of Finance.* Franklin, IN: Southwestern Co., 1975.

Sweeney, Allen and John N. Wisner, Jr., *Budgeting Fundamentals for Nonfinancial Executives.* New York: American Management Associations, 1976.

Sweeny, Allen, *ROI Basics for Nonfinancial Executives.* New York: American Management Associations, 1980.

Decision Management

Nickerson, Charles A. and Ingeborg A. Nickerson, *Statistical Analysis for Decision Making.* New York: PBI-Petrocelli Books, 1979.

Odiorne, George S., *Management Decisions by Objectives*. Englewood Cliffs, NJ: Prentice-Hall, 1969.

Oxenfeldt, Alfred R., et al., *A Basic Approach to Executive Decision Making*. New York: American Management Associations, 1979.

Oxenfeldt. Alfred R., *Cost Benefit Analysis for Executive Decision Making*. New York: American Managment Associations, 1979.

Robertshaw, Joseph E., et al., *Problem Solving: A Systems Approach*. New York: Petrocelli Books, 1979.

Shull, Fremont A., et al., *Organizational Decision Making*. New York: McGraw-Hill, 1970.

Leadership

Bennis, Warren, *The Unconscious Conspiracy: Why Leaders Can't Lead*. New York: American Management Associations, 1976.

Blake, Robert R. and Jane S. Mouton, *The New Managerial Grid*. Houston, TX: Gulf Publishing Co., 1978.

Brown, J. Douglas, *The Human Nature of Organizations*. New York: American Management Associations, 1973.

Cribbin, James J., *Effective Managerial Leadership*. New York: American Management Associations, 1972.

Flory, Charles D., *Managers of Tomorrow*. New York: New American Library, 1971.

Goble, Frank, *Excellence in Leadership*. New York: American Management Associations, 1972.

Green, Richard M., Jr., *The Management Game: How to Win With People*. New York: Dow Jones/Irwin, Inc. 1969.

Grossman, Lee, *The Change Agent*. New York: American Management Associations, 1974.

Hershey, Paul and Kenneth H. Blanchard, *Management of Organizational Behavior*. Englewood Cliffs, NJ: Prentice-Hall, 1977.

Humble, John, *How to Manage by Objectives*. New York: American Management Associations, 1973.

Likert, Rensis, *The Human Organization: Its Management and Value*. New York: McGraw-Hill, 1967.

McConkey, Dale D., *How to Manage by Results*. New York: American Management Associations, 1976.

McConkey, Dale D., *Management by Objectives for Staff Managers*. New York: Vantage Press, 1972.

McGregor, Douglas, *The Human Side of Enterprise*. New York: McGraw-Hill, 1960.

McGregor, Douglas, *The Professional Manager*. New York: McGraw-Hill, 1967.

Maher, John R., ed., *New Perspectives in Job Enrichment.* New York: Van Nostrand Reinhold, 1971.

Mali, Paul, *Managing by Objectives.* New York: Wiley-Interscience, 1972.

Mason, Joseph G., *How to Build Your Management Skills.* New York: McGraw-Hill, 1971.

Merry, Uril and Melvin E. Allerhand, *Developing Teams and Organizations: A Practical Handbook for Managers and Consultants.* Reading, MA: Addison-Wesley, 1977.

Reeves, Elton T., *The Dynamics of Group Behaviour.* New York: American Management Associations, 1970.

Sayles, Leonard R., *Leadership: What Effective Managers Really Do...and How They Do It.* New York: McGraw-Hill, 1979.

Schleh, E., *The Management Tactician: Executive Tactics for Getting Results.* New York: McGraw-Hill, 1974.

Stogdill, Ralph M., *Handbook of Leadership.* New York: Free Press, 1974.

Vardaman, George T., *Dynamics of Managerial Leaderhip.* Pensauken, NJ: Auerbach Publishers, 1973.

Walters, Roy, W., et al., *Job Enrichment for Results: Strategies for Successful Implementation.* Reading, MA: Addison-Wesley, 1975.

Yorks, Lyle, *A Radical Approach to Job Enrichment.* New York: American Management Associations, 1976.

MEDIA MANAGEMENT

Allen Costa, Sylvia, *How to Prepare a Production Budget for Film and Videotape.* Blue Summit, PA: Tab Books, 1975.

Aspen Handbook on Media. 1975-76 ed., Palo Alto, CA: Aspen Institute, 1975.

Baker, H. Ken, "Management by Objectives and How to Implement It." *Public Telecommunication Review,* January-February 1977, pp.18-28.

Belmore, W.E., "The Application Of A Cost Analysis Methodology to the Design Phase of Instructional Development." Ph.D. dissertation, Indiana University, 1972.

Brush, Judith M. and Douglas P., *Private Television Communications: An Awakening Giant.* New Providence, NJ: International Industrial Television Association, 1977.

Bunyan, John, James Crimmins and N. Kyri Watson, *Practical Video: The Manager's Guide to Applications.* White Plains, NY: Knowledge Industry Publications, Inc., 1978.

Bunyan, John and James Crimmins, *Television and Management: The*

Manager's Guide to Video. White Plains, NY: Knowledge Industry Publications, Inc., 1977.

Caffarella, Edward, Jr., "The Cost Effectiveness of Instructional Media Technology in Higher Education." *Educational Technology,* August 1977, pp.23-25.

Caffarella, Edward, Jr., "How Little Do We Know About the Cost-Effectiveness of Instructional Technology?" *Educational Technology,* January 1975, pp.56-58.

Denova, Charles C., *Establishing a Training Function: A Guide for Management.* Englewood Cliffs, NJ: Educational Technology Publications, 1971.

Dranov, Paula, Louise Moore and Adrienne Hickey, *Video in the 80s: Emerging Uses for Television in Business, Education, Medicine and Government.* White Plains, NY: Knowledge Industry Publications, Inc., 1980.

Foltz, Roy G., *Management by Communication.* Radnor, PA: Chilton Book Co., 1975.

Gallup, David A., et al., "Establishing and Administering an Effective Instructional Hardware Distribution Program." *Audiovisual Instruction.* October 1975, pp.18-19.

Gallup, David A., "The Development and Implementation of Model for Comparing Instructional Alternatives." Ph.D dissertation, Pennsylvania State University, 1974.

Harrison, Helen P., *Film Library Techniques: Principles of Administration.* New York: Hastings House, 1973.

Howey, Mary Lou, "Production Cost Analysis." *Educational Television,* November 1970, pp. 26-30.

Hoye, Robert, "Systems Management: The Media Program." *Audiovisual Instruction,* October 1975, pp. 6-7.

Marlow, Eugene, *Communications and the Corporation.* New York: United Business Publications, 1978.

Naval Training Analysis and Evaluation Group, *A Technique for Choosing Cost Effective Instructional Delivery Systems.* Final report, Orlando, FL: Naval Training Equipment Center, ERIC Clearinghouse: ED 111 350.

Planning and Operating Media Centers. Washington, DC: AECT Publications, 1975.

Schmid, W.T., *Cost Accounting — Production and Equipment Services.* ERIC Clearinghouse: ED 122 842.

Schmidt, William T., *Media Center Management: A Practical Guide.* New York: Hastings House, 1980.

Stormes, John M. and James P. Crumpler, *Television Communications Systems for Business and Industry.* New York: Wiley-Interscience, 1970.

The Video Register. White Plains, NY: Knowledge Industry Publications, Inc., 1979.

PUBLIC RELATIONS

Bernays, Edward L., *Biography of an Idea.* New York: Simon & Schuster, 1965.

Bernays, Edward L., *Public Relations.* Norman, OK: University of Oklahoma Press, 1952.

Black, Sam, *Practical Public Relations.* London: Pitman, 1976.

Blumenthal, L.R., *The Practice of Public Relations.* New York: Macmillan, 1972.

Canfield and Moore, *Public Relations: Principles, Cases, Problems.* Homewood, IL: Richard D. Irwin, 1979.

Center, Allen, *Public Relations Practices: Case Studies.* Englewood Cliffs, NJ: Prentice-Hall, 1975.

Jefkins, Frank, *Planned Press and Public Relations.* London: Intertext, 1977

Kadon, A., *Successful Public Relations Techniques.* Modern Schools, Box 8, Scottsdale, AZ, 85251, 1976.

Lesly, Philip, *Lesly's Public Relations Handbook.* Englewood Cliffs, NJ: Prentice-Hall, 1978.

Marston, John, *Modern Public Relations.* New York: McGraw-Hill, 1979.

Newsom and Scott, *This is PR: Realities of Public Relations.* Belmont, CA: Wadsworth Publishing Co., 1976.

Nolte, L.W., *Fundamentals of Public Relations.* Elmsford, NY: Pergamon Press, 1979.

Ross, R.D., *Management of Public Relations.* New York: John Wiley & Sons, 1978.

Simon, R., *Perspectives in Public Relations.* Norman, OK: University of Oklahoma Press, 1966.

Simon, R., *Public Relations: Concepts and Practice.* Columbus, OH: Grid Publishing, 1976.

Simon, R., *Public Relations Management: Cases/Simulations.* Columbus, OH: Grid Publishing, 1977.

Simon, R. *Publicity and Public Relations Worktext.* Columbus, OH: Grid Publishing, 1978.

Steinberg, C., *Creation of Consent: Public Relations In Practice.* New York: Hastings House, 1976.

Stephenson, Howard, *Handbook of Public Relations.* New York: McGraw-Hill, 1971.

TRAINING & DEVELOPMENT

Anderson, Ronald, *Selecting and Developing Media for Instruction.* New York: Van Nostrand Reinhold, 1977.

Baker, Robert, et al., *Instructional Product Development.* New York: Van Nostrand Reinhold, 1971.

Banathy, Bela H., *Instructional Systems.* Belmont, CA: Fearon-Pitman Publishing Co., 1968.

Bell, Norman R. and Allan J. Abedor, *Developing Audio-Visual Instructional Modules for Vocational and Technical Training.* Englewood Cliffs, NJ: Educational Technology Publications Inc., 1977.

Benne, Kenneth D., Leland P. Bradford, Jack R. Gibb and Ronald O. Lippitt, eds., *The Laboratory Method of Changing and Learning: Theory and Application.* Palo Alto, CA: Science and Behavior Books, 1975.

Blake, Robert R., and Jane Srygley Mouton, *Consultation.* Reading, MA: Addison-Wesley, 1976.

Bloom, Benjamin S., et al., *A Taxonomy of Educational Objectives: Handbook I, the Cognitive Domain.* New York: Longmans, Green, 1956.

Bloom, B.S., J.T. Hastings and G.F. Madaus, *Handbook on Formative and Summative Evaluation of Student Learning.* New York: McGraw-Hill, 1971.

Borg, W.R. and P. Hood, *The Twenty-Seven Steps in the Development Program.* Berkeley, CA: Far West Laboratory for Educational Research & Development, 1968.

Briggs, L., *Handbook of Procedures for the Design of Instruction.* Pittsburgh, PA: American Institutes for Research, 1970.

Broadwell, Martin M., *The Supervisor and On-the-Job Training.* Reading, MA: Addison-Wesley, 1975.

Broadwell, Martin M., *The Supervisor As An Instructor: A Guide for Classroom Training.* Reading, MA: Addison-Wesley, 1975.

Brown, James, Richard Lewis and Frederick Harcleroad, *AV Instruction: Technology, Media and Methods.* 4th ed., New York: McGraw-Hill, 1973.

Canfield, Albert A., "A Rationale for Performance Objectives." *Audiovisual Instruction,* February, 1968, pp. 127-29.

Carpenter, P., "Developing a Methodology for Designing Systems of Instruction." *SRIS Quarterly 6 (2)* (Summer 1973).

Cavert, Edward, *An Approach to Design of Mediated Instruction,* Washington, DC: Association for Educational Communications and Technology, 1974.

Colton, F.V. and H. Caton, "Self-Styled Approach to Instructional Design." *Audiovisual Instruction* 19 (10) (December, 1974).

Contributions of Behavioral Sciences to Instructional Technology: Affective Domain. Washington, DC: Communications Service Corp., 1970.

Contributions of Behavioral Science to Instructional Technology: Psychomotor Domain. Washington, DC: Communications Service Corp., 1970.

Craig, Robert L., ed., *Training and Development Handbook: A Guide to Human Resource Development.* 2nd ed. New York: McGraw-Hill, 1976.

Crawford, J., ed., *National Research Training Manual.* 2nd ed. Monmouth, OR: Teaching Research, 1969.

Davis, Larry N. and Earl McCallon, *Planning, Conducting, Evaluating Workshops: A Practitioner's Guide to Adult Education.* Austin, TX: Learning Concepts Publishing Co., 1974.

Designing Effective Instruction Workbook. San Rafael, CA: General Programmed Teaching, 1970.

Donaldson, Les and Edward E. Scannell, *Human Resource Development: The New Trainer's Guide.* Reading, MA: Addison-Wesley, 1978.

Dyer, William G., *Team Building: Issues and Alternatives.* Reading, MA: Addison-Wesley, 1977.

Edling, Jack V., "Educational Objectives and Educational Media." *Review of Educational Research,* April 1968, pp.177-194.

Emery, F.E. ed., *Systems Thinking.* New York: Penguin Publishers, 1969.

Erickson, Carlton, *Administering Instructional Media Programs.* New York: Macmillan, 1968.

Faris, G., "Would You Believe an Instructional Developer." *Audiovisual Instruction* 13 (9) (November 1968).

Finkel, Coleman, *Professional Guide to Successful Meetings.* Philadelphia, PA: SM Book Co., 1976.

Flanagan, J.C., "Functional Education for the Seventies." *Phi Delta Kappan* 49 (1967).

Fordyce, Kack K. and Raymond Weil, *Managing With People: A Manager's Handbook of Organization Development Methods.* 2nd ed. Reading, MA: Addison-Wesley, 1979.

Gage, G. *A Model for Establishing a Priority of Educational Needs.* Monmouth, OR: Teaching Research. February 1970.

Gagne, R.M., *Psychological Principles in System Development*. New York: Holt, Rinehart and Winston, 1962.

Gagne, Robert M. and Leslie J. Briggs, *Principles of Instructional Design*. New York: Holt, Rinehart and Winston, 1974.

Geis, George L., *Behavioral Objectives: A Selected Bibliography and Brief Review*. Palo Alto, CA: Stanford University, ERIC Clearinghouse on Media and Technology, 1972.

Gerlach, V.S. and D.P. Ely, *Teaching and Media: A Systematic Approach*. Englewood Cliffs, NJ: Prentice-Hall, 1970.

Gilbert, T.F., "Mathematics: The Technology of Education." *Journal of Mathematics* 1(1) (1962).

Glaser, R., "Psychological Bases for Instructional Design." *AV Communication Review* 14 (1966).

Gronlund, Norman E., *Stating Behavioral Objectives for Classroom Instruction*, New York: Macmillan, 1970.

Hamreus, D.G., "The Systems Approach to Instructional Development." In *The Contribution of Behavioral Science to Instructional Technology*. Monmouth, OR: Teaching Reasearch, 1968.

Hemphill, J.K., "Management and Operation of Educational Laboratories." *Journal of Research and Development in Education* 3 (2) (1970).

Hernandez, David E., *Writing Behavioral Objectives*. New York: Barnes & Noble, 1971.

Hitchens, H.B., Jr., "Instructional Development: By Design or By Change?" *Audiovisual Instruction* 17 (8) (October 1972).

Ingalls, John D., *Human Energy, the Critical Factor for Individuals and Organizations*. Reading, MA: Addison-Wesley, 1976.

Johnson, M., "The Translation of Curriculum to Instruction," In Taylor, Morris and Kerr, eds., *Journal of Curriculum Studies* 1 (2) (1969).

Kemp, Jerrold E., *Instructional Design: A Plan for Unit and Course Development*. Belmont, CA: Fearon-Pitman Publishing Co., 1977.

Kibler, Robert J., et al., *Behavioral Objectives and Instruction*, Boston, MA: Allyn & Bacon, 1970.

Kiesling, H.J., "On the Economic Analysis of Educational Technology." In Tickton, ed., *To Improve Learning*. Vol. 2. New York: R.R. Bowker, 1971.

Kirkpatrick, Donald, L., *A Practical Guide For Supervisory Training and Development*. Reading, MA: Addison-Wesley, 1971.

Kirkpatrick, Donald L., *Evaluating Training Programs: A Collection of Articles for the Journal of the American Society for Training and Development*. Madison, WI: American Society for Training and Development, 1975.

Kirkpatrick, Donald L., *How to Plan and Conduct Productive Business Meetings.* Chicago, IL: Dartnell Corp., 1976.

Knowles, Malcolm S., *Self-Directed Learning: A Guide for Learners and Teachers.* New York: Association Press, 1975.

Krathwohl, David R., et al., *A Taxonomy of Educational Objectives Handbook II, the Affective Domain.* New York: David McKay Co., 1964.

Kryspin, William J. and John F. Feldhusin, *Writing Behavioral Objectives.* Minneapolis, MN: Burgess Publishing Co., 1974.

Laird, Dugan, *A User's Look at the Audio-Visual World.* 2nd ed. Fairfax, VA: The National Audio-Visual Associaton, 1974.

Laird, Dugan, *Approaches to Training and Development.* Reading, MA: Addison-Wesley, 1978.

Leedham, John, *The Imaginative Use of Closed Circuit TV in Training of Staff and Managers.* Report to UNESCO by the Association for Programmed Learning and Educational Technology. ERIC Clearinghouse: ED 140 785.

Lehmann, H., "Systems Approach to Education." *Audiovisual Instruction* 13 (2) (1968).

Lippitt, Gordon, L., *Visualizing Change: Model Building and the Change Process.* Fairfax, VA: NTL Learning Resources Corp., 1973.

Lippitt, Gordon and Bernard Taylor, eds., *Management Development and Training Handbook.* London, New York: McGraw-Hill, 1975.

Mager, Robert F. and Peter Pipe, *Analyzing Performance Problems: Or, You Really Oughta Wanna.* Belmont, CA: Fearon-Pitman Publishing Co., 1970.

Mager, Robert F., *Developing Vocational Instruction.* Belmont, CA: Fearon-Pitman Publishing Co., 1967.

Mager, Robert F., *Goal Analysis.* Belmont, CA: Fearon Lear/Siegler, 1971.

Mager, Robert F., *Measuring Instructional Intent: Or, Got A Match?* Belmont, CA: Fearon-Pitman Publishing Co., 1973.

Mager, Robert F., *Preparing Instructional Objectives.* 2nd ed. Belmont, CA: Fearon-Pitman Publishing Co., 1975.

Moore, J.W., "A Program for Systematic Instructional Improvement." *Audiovisual Instruction* 15 (2) (February 1970).

Morris, W.T., *The Analysis of Management Decisions.* Rev. ed. Homewood, IL: Richard D. Irwin, 1964.

Nadler, David A., *Feedback and Organization Development: Using Data-Based Methods.* Reading, MA: Addison-Wesley, 1977.

Nadler, Leonard, *Developing Human Resources.* Houston, TX: Gulf Publishing Co., 1970.

National Special Media Institute, *Instructional Development Institute.*

U.S. Office of Education, Bureau of Libraries and Educational Technology, Division of Education Technology, Media Specialist Program, 1971.

Odiorne, George S., *Training By Objectives: An Economic Approach to Training.* New York: Macmillan, 1970.

Pfeiffer, J. William and John E. Jones, eds., *The Annual Handbook for Group Facilitators.* La Jolla, CA: University Associates Press, 1972-1977.

Pinnell, C. and M. Wacholder, *Guidelines for Planning in Colleges and Universities.* Austin, TX: Texas College and University System, 1968.

Plowman, Paul D., *Behavioral Objectives.* Chicago, IL: Science Research Associates, 1971.

Popham, W.J. and E.L. Baker, "Rules for the Development of Instructional Products." *The Staff Development Compendium.* New York: Van Nostrand-Reinhold, 1971.

Roman, D.D., *Research and Development Management: The Economics and Administration of Technology.* New York: Appleton-Century-Crofts, 1968.

Schutz, R.E., "The Nature of Educational Development." *Journal of Research and Development in Education* 3 (2) (1970).

Smith, R.G., *An Annotated Bibliography on the Design of Instructional Systems.* Alexandria, VA: Human Resources Research Office, George Washington University, 1967.

Smith, Robert G., *Controlling the Quality of Training.* Alexandria, VA: Human Resources Research Office, George Washington University, 1965.

Smith, Robert G., *The Development of Training Objectives.* Alexandria, VA: Human Resources Research Office, George Washington Unversity, 1964.

Southwest Regional Laboratory for Educational Research and Development, *Teacher's Manual - SWRL First-Year Communication Skills Program.* Inglewood, CA: SWRL for Educational Research and Development, 1969.

Stowe, R.A., ed., *Case Studies in Instructional Development.* Bloomington, IN: Indiana University, Laboratory for Educational Development, School of Education, 1969.

Stowe, R.A., "Research and the Systems Approach as Methodologies for Education." *AV Communication Review* 21 (2) (Summer 1973).

Tickton, Sidney, G., ed., *To Improve Learning: An Evaluation of Instructional Technology.* From a report to the President and Congress by the Commission on Instructional Technology. New York: R.R. Bowker, 1970.

Training Analysis and Evaluation Group, *Designing of Training Systems, Phase 2 - A Report, An Educational Technology Assessment*

Model, Final Report. Orlando, FL: Naval Training Equipment Center, ERIC Clearinghouse: ED 112 892.

Twelker, P.A., F.D. Urbach and J.E. Buck, *The Systematic Development of Instruction: An Overview and Basic Guide to the Literature.* Corvallis, OR: United States International University in Oregan, 1972.

Unwin, Derick and Ray McAleese, eds., *Encyclopedia of Educational Media Communications and Technology.* Westport, CT: Greenwood Press, 1978.

Varney, Glenn H., *Organization Development for Managers.* Reading, MA: Addison-Wesley, 1977.

Voegel, G.H., ed., "Instructional Development: An Emerging Process." *Audiovisual Instruction* 16 (10) (December 1971).

Zaltman, G. and N. Lin, "On the Nature of Innovations." *American Behavioral Scientist* 14 (1971).

VIDEO/FILM/MULTIMEDIA PRODUCTION

Arnheim, Rudolf, *Art and Visual Perception.* Berkeley, CA: University of California Press, 1954.

Baddeley, W. Hugh, *The Technique of Documentary Film Production.* New York: Hastings House, 1973.

Barnouw, Erik, *The Television Writer.* New York: Hill and Wang, 1962.

Beeler, Duane and Frank McCallister, *Creative Use of Films in Education.* Chicago, IL: Roosevelt University, Labor Education Division, 1968.

Benedict, Joel A. and Douglas A. Crane, *Producing Multi-Image Presentations.* Tempe, AZ: Arizona State University, Audiovisual Service, 1973.

Bensinger, Charles, *Peterson's Guide to Video Tape Recording* Los Angeles, CA: Peterson Publishing Co., 1973.

Bension, Samuel, *New York Production Manual.* New York: New York Production Manual, Inc., 1979.

Beveridge, James A., *Script Writing for Short Films.* New York: UNESCO Publishing Center USA, 1969.

Bland, Michael, *The Executive's Guide to TV and Radio Appearances.* White Plains, NY: Knowledge Industry Publications, Inc., 1980.

Bretz, Rudy, *Techniques of Television Production.* 2nd ed., New York: McGraw-Hill, 1962.

Brown, James W., et al., *AV Instruction: Technology, Media, and Methods.* New York: McGraw-Hill, 1973.

Burder, John, *The Work of the Industrial Film Maker.* New York: Hastings House, 1973.

Carroll, J.A. and R.E. Sherriffs, *TV Lighting Handbook*. Blue Ridge Summmit, PA: Tab Books, 1980.

Clarke, Beverly, *Graphic Design in Educational Television*. New York: Watson-Guptill Publications, 1974.

Clarke, Charles G. and Walter Strenge, eds., *American Cinematographer Manual*. Hollywood, CA: American Society of Cinematographers, 1973.

Dale, Edgar, *Audiovisual Methods in Teaching*, 3rd ed., New York: Holt, Rinehart & Winston, 1969.

Davis, Desmond, *The Grammar of Television Production*. London: Barrie & Jenkins, 1974.

Duval County School System, *Graphics Communication - Industrial Arts Performance Objectivies*. ERIC Clearinghouse: ED 139 972.

Efrein, Joel, *Videotape Production and Communication Techniques*. Blue Ridge Summit, PA: Tab Books, 1971.

Frye, Roy, *Graphic Tools for Teachers*. Mapleville, RI: Roy Frye Publications, 1975.

Garland, Ken, *Graphics Handbook*. New York: Van Nostrand Reinhold, 1966.

Gordon, Roger, ed., *The Art of Multi-Image*. Abington, PA: Association for Multi-Image, 1978.

Hall, Joel, *Tape Editing*. Washington, DC: The Editall Corporation, 1980.

Herman, Lewis, *Educational Films: Writing, Directing, and Producing for Classroom, Television, and Industry*. New York: Crown, 1966.

Hurrell, Ron, *Van Nostrand Reinhold Manual of Television Graphics*. New York: Van Nostrand Reinhold, 1973.

Huss, Roy and Norman Silverstein, *The Film Experience — Elements of Motion Picture Art*. New York: Dell, 1968.

Jones, Gary and Phil Squyers, *1973 Electronic Film/Tape Post-Production Handbook*. Dallas, TX: Fratellitre Communications, 1973.

Jones, Peter, *The Technique of the Television Cameraman*. Rev. ed., New York: Hastings House,1972.

Kehoe, Vincent J.,*The Technique of Film and Television Make-up for Color and Black and White*. Rev. ed., New York: Hastings House, 1969.

Kemp, Jerrold E., *Planning and Producing Audio-Visual Materials*. 4th ed., San Francisco, CA: Harper & Row, 1980.

Klein, Walter J., *The Sponsored Film*. New York: Hastings House, 1976.

Kuhns, William and Robert Stanley, *Exploring the Film*. Dayton, OH: Pflaum Press, 1968.

Lee, Robert and Robert Misiorowski, *Script Models: A Handbook for the Media Writer*. New York: Hastings House, 1978.

Lewis, Bruce, *The Technique of Television Announcing.* New York, Hastings House, 1966.

Lewis, Colby, *TV Director/Interpreter.* 4th ed., New York: Hastings House, 1973.

Logan, Ben, ed., *Television Awareness Training.* New York: Media Action Research Center, 1977.

MacLinker, Jerry, *Designing Instructional Visuals: Theory, Composition, and Implementation.* Austin, TX: University of Texas, Instructional Media Center, 1968.

Marsh, Ken, *Independent Video.* San Francisco, CA: Straight Arrow Books, 1974.

Mascelli, Joseph V., *The Five C's of Cinematography.* Hollywood, CA: Cine/Graphics Publications, 1965.

Matrazzo, Donna, *The Corporate Scriptwriting Book.* Philadelphia, PA: Media Concepts, 1980.

Mikolas, Mark and Gunther Hoos, *Handbook of Super 8 Production.* 2nd ed., New York: United Business Publications, 1979.

Millerson, Gerald, *Basic TV Staging.* New York: Hastings House, 1974.

Millerson, Gerald, *TV Camera Operation.* New York: Hasting House, 1973.

Millerson, Gerald, *The Technique of Lighting for Television and*
Millerson, Gerald, *The Technique of Television Production.* 13th ed. New York: Hastings House, 1977.

Minor, Ed , et al., *Techniques for Producing Visual Instructional Media.* New York: McGraw-Hill, 1970.

Murray, Michael, *The Videotape Book: A Basic Guide to Portable TV Production.* New York: Taplinger Publishing Co., 1975.

Oringel, Robert F., *Audio Control Handbook for Radio and TV Broadcasting.* New York: Hastings House, 1972.

Parker, Ben, et al., *Creative Intention: About Audiovisual Communication.* New York: Law-Arts Publishing Co., 1974.

Pincus, Edward, *Guide to Filmmaking.* New York: New American Library, 1969.

Rehrauer, George, *The Film User's Handbook.* New York: R.R. Bowker, 1979.

Reisz, Karel and Gavin Millar, *The Technique of Film Editing.* New York: Hastings House, 1964.

Rivers, William, *The Mass Media: Reporting, Writing, Editing.* New York: Harper & Row, 1975.

Robinson, Richard, *The Video Primer: Equipment, Production and Concepts.* New York: Quick Fox, 1978.

Rosien, Arthur H., ed., *The Video Handbook*. 3rd ed. New York: United Business Publications, 1979.

Rowe, Mack R., et al., *The Message Is You: Guidelines for Preparing Presentations*. Washington, DC: Association for Educational Communications and Technology, 1971.

Samuelson, David W., *Motion Picture Camera and Lighting Equipment*. New York: Hastings House, 1977.

Schroeppel, Tom, *The Bare Bones Camera Course for Film and Video*. Miami, FL: Tom Schroeppel, Dept. V.P.O. Box 521110, Miami, FL 33152.

Schwartz, Tony, *The Responsive Chord*. Garden City, NY: Anchor Press, 1973.

Smith, Todd and Jim Aneshansley, *The Oxberry Slide Handbook*. Carlstadt, NJ: Oxberry, 1980.

Spear, John, *Creating Visuals for Television*. Washington, DC: National Educational Association, 1962.

Spottiswoode, Raymond, ed., *The Focal Encyclopedia of Film and Television Techniques*. New York: Hastings House, 1969.

Stasheff, Edward and Rudy Brets, *The Television Program: Its Direction and Production*. New York: Hill and Wang, 1968.

Stone, Vernon and Bruce Hinson, *Television Newsfilm Techniques*. New York: Hastings House, 1974.

The Video Source Book. Syosset, NY: The National Clearinghouse, Inc., 1979.

Thompson, Tom, *Organizational TV News*. Philadelphia, PA: Media Concepts, 1980.

Trapnell, Coles, *Teleplay: An Introduction to Television Writing*. New York: Hawthorn Books, 1974.

Videofreek, *The Spaghetti City Video Manual*. New York: Praeger Publishers, 1973.

Westmoreland, Bob, *Teleproduction Shortcuts: A Manual for Low-Budget Television Production in a Small Studio*. Norman, OK: University of Oklahoma Press, 1974.

Wilkie, Bernard, *Creating Special Effects for TV and Films*. New York: Hastings House, 1977.

Wilkie, Bernard, *The Techniques of Special Effects in Television*. New York: Hastings House, 1971.

Williams, Richard, *Television Production: A Vocational Approach*. Salt Lake City, UT: Television Production and Utilization Specialists.

Wolff, Herbert and John Quick, *Small Studio Video Tape Production*. 2nd ed., Reading, MA: Addison-Wesley, 1976.

Wortman, Leon, *Closed Circuit Television Handbook*. Indianapolis, IN: Howard W. Sams & Co., 1974.

Wright, Andrew, *Designing for Visual Aids*. New York: Van Nostrand Reinhold, 1970.

Writers Guild of America, *The Writers' Guild of America Professional Writers' Teleplay/Screenplay Format*. New York: Writers Guild of America East.

Wurtzel, Alan, *Television Production*. New York: McGraw-Hill, 1979.

Zettl, Herbert, *Sight, Sound, Motion*. Belmont, CA: Wadsworth Publishing Co., 1973.

Zettl, Herbert, *Television Production Handbook*. 3rd ed. Belmont, CA: Wadsworth Publishing Co., 1976.

Appendix II: Professional Organizations

AAIM
American Association of Industrial Management
7425 Old York Rd.
Philadelphia, PA 19126
215-657-2100
Companies in electrical, automotive, chemical, paper, insurance, etc., concerned with training, industrial relations research, communications.

AAVT
Association of Audio-Visual Technicians
c/o Damian Appert
Audio-Visual Center
University of California
Davis, CA 95616
916-752-3553
Production technicians — graphic artists, photographers, etc.; equipment and maintenance repair persons.

ABCA
American Business Communication Association
317b David Kinley Hall
University of Illinois
Urbana, IL 61801
217-333-1007
College teachers of business communication and management consultants.

ABWA
Associated Business Writers of America
PO Box 135
Monmouth Junction, NJ 08852
201-297-4891
Professional freelance writers who specialize in business writing.

ACVL
Association of Cinema & Video Laboratories
PO Box 34932
Bethesda, MD 20034
301-469-8881
Motion picture laboratories supplying various services to motion picture producers, agencies, television and the theater.

AECT
Association for Educational Communications & Technology
1126 16th St. NW
Washington, DC 20036
202-833-4180
AV and instructional materials specialists, educational technologists, AV and TV production personnel and educators.

This information is derived primarily from *Encyclopedia of Associations*, edited by Margaret Fisk (Detroit, MI: Gale Research Co., 1977).

AES
Audio Engineering Society
60 E. 42nd St., Room 449
New York, NY 10017
212-661-8528
Engineers, administrators and technicians who design or operate recording equipment for radio, TV, motion picture and recording studios.

AIGA
American Institute of Graphic Arts
1059 Third Ave.
New York, NY 10021
212-752-0813
Graphic artists involved in book design, illustrations, advertising, corporate graphics, promotion and exhibitions.

AIM
American Institute of Management
607 Boylston St.
Boston, MA 02116
617-536-2503
Executives interested in management efficiency and methods of appraising management performance.

AMA
American Management Association
135 W. 50th St.
New York, NY 10020
212-586-8100
Managers in industry, commerce, government.

AMI
Association for Multi-Image
947 Old York Rd.
Abington, PA 19001
215-572-5656
Educators, industrial trainers, media specialists.

AMP
Association of Media Producers
1707 L St. NW, Suite 515
Washington, DC 20036
202-296-4710
Producers and distributors of educational media, materials; companies providing technical or professional services to industry.

ANA
Association of National Advertisers
155 E. 44th St.
New York, NY 10017
212-697-5950
National and regional advertisers; committees on AV and sales promotion.

ASC
American Society of Cinematographers
1782 N. Orange Dr.
Hollywood, CA 90028
213-876-5080
Professional directors of motion picture and television photography; others affiliated with cinematography.

ASFA
American Science Film Association
3624 Science Center
Philadelphia, PA 19104
215-387-2255
Scientists, educators, film producers and distributors using film, TV and related media as tools of research, and for communicating research.

ASIFA
International Animated Film Association
25 W. 43rd St., Room 1018
New York, NY 10036
Exchange information on animated film and technique; support animated film societies.

ASMP
American Society of Magazine Photographers
205 Lexington Ave.
New York, NY 10016
212-889-9144
Maintains and promotes high professional standards and ethics in photography; cultivates mutual understanding among professional photographers.

ASTD
American Society for Training and Development
PO Box 5307
Madison, WI 53705
608-274-3440
Persons engaged in training and development of business, industrial and government personnel.

ASTVC
American Society of TV Cameramen
PO Box 296
Sparkill, NY 10976
914-359-5985
Professional cameramen and persons in related jobs.

AVI
American Video Institute
50 Morningside Dr.
New York, NY 10025
212-864-1415
Institutions and individuals with a special focus on interactive video disc.

AVMA (formerly IAVA)
Audio Visual Management Association
Box 656 Downtown Station
Chicago, IL 60690
Managers of AV departments of business and industrial firms.

AWRT
American Women in Radio & TV
1321 Connecticut Ave. NW
Washington, DC 20036
202-296-0009
Professionals in administrative, creative or executive positions in broadcasting and ad agencies, service organizations, government or charitable agencies devoted to radio and TV.

CCIA
Computer and Communications
  Industry Association
1500 Wilson Blvd., Suite 512
Arlington, VA 22209
703-524-1360
*Mainframe vendors, software and
service houses, leasing and maintenance companies, peripheral
manufacturers.*

CINE
Council on International Non-
  Theatrical Events
1201 16th St. NW
Washington, DC 20036
202-785-1136
*Reviews nontheatrical TV, docu-
mentary, and short subject motion
pictures for redistribution.*

EFLA
Educational Film Library Association
43 W. 61st St.
New York, NY 10023
212-246-4533
*Educational institutions, commer-
cial organizations and individuals
interested in nontheatrical films.
National clearinghouse for information about 16mm films.*

EIA
Electronic Industries Association
2001 Eye St., NW
Washington, DC 20006
202-457-4900
*Manufacturers of radio, TV, video
systems, audio equipment and industrial and communications electronic products.*

GAG (East)
Graphic Artists Guild
30 E. 20th St.
New York, NY 10003
212-982-9298
See GAG (West)

GAG (West)
Bldg. 314, Fort Mason Center
San Francisco, CA 94212
*National organization for com-
mercial artists, illustrators, de-
signers, etc.*

HESCA
Health Science Communications
  Association
2343 N. 115th St.
Wauwatosa, WI 53226
*Media managers, biomedical librar-
ians, producers of programs,
faculty members of health science
schools, industry representatives.*

IABC
International Association of
  Business Communicators
870 Market St., Suite 928
San Francisco, CA 94102
415-433-3400
*Editors of periodicals (industrial,
trade, association) issued regularly
and published for employees,
association members or external
audiences.*

IAIP
International Association of
Independent Producers
PO Box 1933
Washington, DC 20013
202-638-5593
*Persons and firms associated with
all phases of the motion picture
and recording industry.*

IAS
International Audiovisual Society
PO Box Two
Cullowhee, NC 28723
704-293-9026
*Individuals with academic degrees
or equivalent in scientific or tech-
nical experience, with expertise in
AV technology principles.*

ICA
International Communication
    Association
Balcones Research Center
10100 Burnet Rd.
Austin, TX 78758
512-835-3000
*College and university teachers,
businessmen, public relations ad-
visors, etc. interested in communication.*

ICC
Industrial Communication Coun-
    cil
PO Box 3970
Grand Central Station
New York, NY 10017
*Communications specialists within
business and government organi-
zations responsible for establish-
ing policy and directing media.*

IEEE
Institute of Electrical and Elec-
    tronics Engineers
345 E. 47th St.
New York, NY 10017
212-644-7910
*Engineers, scientists and students
in electrical engineering, electronics and allied fields.*

IFPA
Information Film Producers of
    America
750 E. Colorado Blvd.
Pasadena, CA 91101
213-795-7866
*Media producers, managers, crea-
tive and technical people in industry, government and education
dedicated to nontheatrical film
and media communication.*

IGC
Institute for Graphic Communi-
    cation
375 Commonwealth Ave.
Boston, MA 02115
617-267-9425
*Persons interested in graphic com-
munications technologies and markets.*

IGI
Industrial Graphics International
PO Box 4146
Huntsville, AL 35802
205-876-4424
*Graphic communicators in indus-
trial, scientific and technical art,
graphic design, motion pictures,
photography and TV using visual
graphics.*

IIA
Information Industry Association
316 Pennsylvania Ave., SE
Washington, DC 20003
202-544-1969
*For profit information companies
whose business is to identify information needs and to produce
products to meet those needs.*

IMS
Industrial Management Society
570 Northwest Hwy.
Des Plaines, IL 60016
312-296-7189
*Production management execu-
tives interested in time and motion
study, methods, production control. Film and AV competition in
education, safety and productivity.*

IQ
International Quorum of Motion
  Picture Producers
PO Box 395
Oakton, VA 22124
703-281-4508
*Nontheatrical motion picture pro-
duction companies specializing in
films for industry, government and
television.*

IRTS
International Radio & TV Society
420 Lexington Ave.
New York,NY 10017
212-867-6650
*Individuals in management, sales,
or executive production in radio
and TV broadcasting industries
and their allied fields.*

ISCET
International Society of Certified
  Electronics Technicians
PO Box 1258, ISU Station
Ames, IA 50010
515-382-6916
*Technicians, mainly in consumer
electronics, certified by the Na-
tional Electronic Service Dealer
Association.*

ITA
International Tape Association
10 W. 66th St.
New York, NY 10023
212-787-0910
*Major manufacturers of home and
institutional audio-video tape and
equipment and supportive industries.*

ITVA
International Television Association
136 Sherman Ave.
Berkeley Heights, NJ 07922
201-464-6747
*Persons engaged in communica-
tions needs analysis, scriptwriting,
producing, directing, operations
and management in nonbroadcast
television.*

IVLA
International Visual Literacy Association
Center for Visual Literacy
Gallaudet College
Kendall Green
Washington, DC 20002
202-651-5000
Professionals in teaching (visual media, early learning), medicine, and television interested in methods of visual communication.

JCET
Joint Council on Educational Telecommunications
1126 16th St., NW
Washington, DC 20036
202-659-9742
Leading communications and educational organizations; coordinates education's interests in communications technology, policy and regulation.

MCEI
Marketing Communications Executives International
2130 Delancey Place
Philadelphia, PA 19103
215-732-9340
Executives engaged in supervision, planning, execution or direction of marketing communications.

NAB
National Association of Broadcasters
1771 N St., NW
Washington, DC 20036
202-293-3500
Radio and TV stations, associate producers of equipment and programs.

NAEB
National Association of Educational Broadcasters
1346 Connecticut Ave. NW
Washington, DC 20036
202-785-1100
Educational television stations, radio stations and individuals.

NAMW
National Association of Media Women
157 W. 126th St.
New York, NY 10027
212-850-1886
Women professionally engaged in mass communications.

NATAS
National Academy of TV Arts and Sciences
110 W. 57th St.
New York, NY 10019
Persons actively engaged in TV performing, art direction, taping, tape editing, etc.

NAVA
National Audio Visual Association
3150 Spring St.
Fairfax, VA 22030
703-273-7200
Dealers, manufacturers, producers and suppliers of AV products and materials.

NCA
National Cable TV Association
918 16th St., NW
Washington, DC 20006
202-457-6700
Cable TV systems, cable and equipment manufacturers, distributors, brokerage firms and financial institutions.

NCA
National Composition Association
1730 N. Lynn St.
Arlington, VA 22209
703-841-8100
Typesetting, word processing, computerized equipment users.

NCTI
National Cable TV Institute
PO Box 27277
Denver, CO 80227
303-697-4967
Provides technical educational material for the cable TV industry.

NFLPA
National Free Lance Photographers Association
Four E. State St.
Doylestown, PA 18901
215-348-2990
Amateur and professional photographers. Maintains photographic file for industry members.

NY/IABC
New York/International Association of Business Communicators
c/o George Stoddard
Metropolitan Life Insurance
One Madison Ave.
New York, NY 10010
212-578-3032
Editors of company publications, communications specialists, managers of communications programs.

PCNY
The Publicity Club of New York
404 Park Ave., Suite 1207
New York, NY 10016
212-685-8220
Working publicists and public relations executives.

POPAI
Point-of-Purchase Advertising Institute
60 E. 42nd St.
New York, NY 10017
212-682-7091
Producers and suppliers of point-of-purchase advertising signs and displays. Retailers interested in use and effectiveness of point-of-purchase media are associate members.

PPA
Professional Photographers of
America, Inc.
1090 Executive Way
Des Plaines, IL 60018
312-299-8161
Portrait, commercial and industrial photographers. Includes the American Photographic Artisan's Guild and the American Society of Photographers.

PRSA
Public Relations Society of
America
845 Third Ave.
New York, NY 10022
212-826-1750
Public relations practitioners in business and industry, counseling firms, trade and professional groups, government, education, health and welfare organizations.

SALT
Society for Applied Learning
50 Culpeper St.
Warrenton, VA 22186
803-347-0055
Senior executives from military academic and industrial organizations which design, manufacture, or use training technology including audiovisual instruction delivery devices.

SMPTE
Society of Motion Picture and
Television Engineers
862 Scarsdale Ave.
Scarsdale, NY 10583
914-472-6606
Professional engineers and technicians in motion picture, television and allied arts and sciences.

STC
Society for Technical Communication
1010 Vermont Ave. NW, Suite 421
Washington, DC 20005
202-737-0035
Educators, scientists, engineers, artists and others, professionally engaged in corporate technical communications.

TIA (formerly ITCA)
Typographers International
Association
2262 Hall Place
Washington, DC 20007
Typographic companies serving printers, publishers, advertising agencies, art studios, government, institutions and buyers of typographic composition and related products and services.

TMDA
Training Media Distributors
Association
1258 N. Highland Ave., Suite 102
Los Angeles, CA 90038
213-469-6030
Producers and distributors of audiovisual training materials.

VPA
Videotape Production Association
63 W. 83rd St.
New York, NY 10024
212-935-2220
Videotape production firms, suppliers of videotape personnel and facilities. Manufacturers, distributors and suppliers of videotape equipment are associate members.

WGA
Writers Guild of America
8955 Beverly Blvd.
Los Angeles, CA 90048
213-550-1000
Labor union for writers in motion pictures, TV and radio.

WICI
Women in Communications, Inc.
PO Box 9561
Austin, TX 78766
512-345-8922
Women in journalism, public relations and communications.

WID
Women in Design
530 Howard St.
San Francisco, CA 94107
Women designers in the graphic arts.

Appendix III: Trade and Professional Periodicals

Advertising Age
Crain Communications, Inc.
740 North Rush
Chicago, IL 60611

Advertising Techniques
Advertising Trade Publication
19 W. 44th St.
New York, NY 10036

American Cinematographer
American Society of Cinematographers Corp.
1782 N. Orange Dr.
Hollywood, CA 90028

American Photographer
Image-Nation Co.
111 Eighth Ave.
New York, NY 10011

Art Direction
Advertising Trade Publication
19 W. 44th St.
New York, NY 10036

Audio
North American Publishing Co.
401 N. Broad St.
Philadelphia, PA 19108

Audiovideo International
Dempa Publications, Inc.
380 Madison Ave.
New York, NY 10017

Audio-Visual Communications
United Business Publications, Inc.
475 Park Ave. S.
New York, NY 10016

Audiovisual Instruction
AECT-Association for Educational Communications &
Technology
1126 16th St. NW
Washington, DC 20036

Audio Visual News Briefs
Association of National Advertisers
155 E. 44th St.
New York, NY 10017

Audio Visual Product News
Montage Publishing
1176 Westminster Ave., Suite B
Los Angeles, CA 90034

Back Stage
Back Stage Publications
165 W. 46th St.
New York, NY 10036

The Balance Sheet
South-Western Publishing Co.
Madison Rd.
Cincinnati, OH 45227

Billboard
Billboard Publications, Inc.
165 W. 46th St.
New York, NY 10036

Biomedical Communications
United Business Publications, Inc.
475 Park Ave. S.
New York, NY 10016

Broadcast Engineering
Intertec Publishing Corp.
Box 12901
Overland Park, KS 66212

Broadcast Management/Engineering
Broadband Information Services, Inc.
295 Madison Ave.
New York, NY 10017

Broadcasting Magazine
Broadcasting Publications, Inc.
1735 DeSales St. NW
Washington, DC 20036

Business Screen
Back Stage Publications
165 W. 46th St.
New York, NY 10036

Camera 35
420 Lexington Ave.
New York, NY 10017

The Camera Craftsman
National Camera
Englewood, CO 80110

Close-up
Polaroid Corp.
549 Technology Square
Cambridge, MA 02139

Communication Arts
Coyne & Blachard Inc.
410 Sherman Ave.
Palo Alto, CA 94303

Communications News
Harcourt Brace Jovanovich
402 West Liberty
Wheaton, IL 60187

The Communicator
IFPA Film & Video Communicators
3518 Cahuenga Blvd. W.
Suite 313
Hollywood, CA 90068

Corporate Public Issues
Geyer-McAllister Publications
51 Madison Ave.
New York, NY 10010

Current Management
Bureau of Business Practice
24 Rope Ferry Rd.
Waterford, CT 06386

DB-The Sound Engineering Magazine
Sagamore Publishing Co., Inc.
1120 Old Country Rd.
Plainview, NY 11803

Dignan Photographic Inc.
12304 Erwin St.
North Hollywood, CA 91606

Donnybrook Report: Photography
3 Grove Court
New York, NY 10014

Educational and Industrial Television
Tepfer Publishing
51 Sugar Hollow Rd.
Danbury, CT 06810

Electronic Industry Weekly
254 W. 31st St.
New York, NY 10001

Electro-Optical Systems Design
Milton S. Kiver Publications, Inc.
222 W. Adams St.
Chicago, IL 60606

ETV Newsletter
C.S. Tepfer Publishing Co.
PO Box 565
Ridgefield, CT 06877

The Executive Manager
American Association of Industrial Management
7425 Old York Rd.
Philadelphia, PA 19126

Film News
Film News Co.
250 W. 57th St.
New York, NY 10019

Filmmakers: Film and Video Monthly
Suncraft International, Inc.
PO Box 115
Ward Hill, MA 01830

Functional Photography
PTN Publishing Corp.
250 Fulton Ave.
Hempstead, NY 11550

The Gallagher Report
Bernard P. Gallagher
230 Park Ave.
New York, NY 10017

Graphic Arts News
CAE Co.
3950 Campus Dr.
Newport Beach, CA 92660

Graphic Design+
Orion Books, Museum Books, Inc.
48 E. 43rd St.
New York, NY 10017

The Gibson Report
D. Parke Gibson International Inc.
475 Fifth Ave.
New York, NY 10017

Graphics Today
Syndicate Magazines
6 E. 43rd St.
New York, NY 10017

Graphic: The International Journal for Graphic and Applied Arts
The Graphic Press
107 Dufourstrasse
CH8008 Zurich, Switzerland

c/o Hastings House Publishers
10 E. 40th St.
New York, NY 10016

Graphics: USA
Kaye Publishing Corp.
120 E. 56th St.
New York, NY 10022

Harvard Business Review
Harvard University
Graduate School of Business Administration
Soldiers Field
Boston, MA 02163

Home Video
United Business Publications,
   Inc.
475 Park Ave. S.
New York, NY 10016

Idea
Museum Books, Inc.
48 E. 43rd St.
New York, NY 10017

Industrial Marketing
Crain Communications, Inc.
740 Rush St.
Chicago, IL 60611

Industrial Photography
United Business Publications Inc.
475 Park Ave. S.
New York, NY 10016

**The Inland Printer/American
Lithographer**
Maclean-Hunter Publishing Corp.
300 W. Adams St.
Chicago, IL 60606

Instructional Innovator
AECT
1126 16th St. NW
Washington, DC 20036

International Photo Technik
H.P. Marketing Corp.
98 Commerce Rd.
Cedar Grove, NJ 07009

International Photographer
International Alliance of
   Theatrical State Employees
   and Moving Picture Machine
   Operators
7715 Sunset Blvd.
Hollywood, CA 90046

Jack O'Dwyer's PR Newsletter
J.R. O'Dwyer Co., Inc.
271 Madison Ave.
New York, NY 10016

**Journal of Applied Photographic
Engineering**
Society of Photographic
   Scientists and Engineers
1411 K Street NW
Suite 930
Washington, DC 20005

**Journal of the Biological Photog-
raphers Association**
1740 Salt Rd.
Rochester, NY 14450

Journal of Communication
International Communication
   Association
Balcones Research Center
10100 Burnet Rd.
Austin, TX 78758

**Journal of Educational
Technology Systems**
Society for Applied Learning
   Technology
50 Culpeper St.
Warrenton, VA 22186

Journal of Micrographics
National Micrographic
  Association
8728 Colesville Rd.
Silver Spring , MD 20910

Management Digest
American Management
  Association
135 W. 50th St.
New York, NY 10020

Marketing Communications
United Business Publications Inc.
475 Park Ave. S.
New York, NY 10016

The Media Communicator
ASTD-American Society for
  Training and Development
Box 5307
Madison, WI 53705

Media Decisions
Decisions Publications, Inc.
342 Madison Ave.
New York, NY 10020

Media History Digest
Media History Digest, Inc.
Philadelphia, PA 19126

Media Industry Newsletter
MIN Publishing Co.
150 E. 52nd St.
New York, NY 10022

Microfilm Techniques
PTN Publishing Corp.
250 Fulton Ave.
Hempstead, NY 11550

Millimeter Magazine
Millimeter Magazine, Inc.
12 E. 46th St.
New York, NY 10017

Modern Lithography
4 Second Ave.
Danville, ND 07834

Modern Photography
Leisure Magazines, Inc.
130 E. 59th St.
New York, NY 10022

Multi-Images Journal
Association for Multi-Image
947 Old York Rd.
Abington, PA 19001

Optical Engineering
Society of Photo-Optical Instru-
  mentation Engineers
PO Box 10
405 Fieldston Rd.
Bellingham, WA 98225

On Location
Consoldiated Publishing, Inc.
6464 Sunset Blvd., Suite 570
Hollywood, CA 90038

Panorama
Triangle Communications, Inc.
850 Third Ave.
New York, NY 10022

**Photogrammetric Engineering
and Remote Sensing**
American Society of
  Photogrammetry
105N Virginia Ave.
Falls Church, VA 22046

**Photographic Science and
Engineering**
Society of Photographic Scientists
& Engineers
Suite 930
1411 K St. NW
Washington, DC 20005

Photographic Trade News
PTN Publishing Corp.
250 Fulton Ave.
Hempstead, NY 11550

Photomethods
Ziff-Davis Publishing Co.
One Park Ave.
New York, NY 10016

The Photo Reporter
319 E. 44th St.
New York, NY 10017

Popular Photography
Ziff-Davis Publishing Co.
One Park Ave.
New York, NY 10016

PR Aids' Party Line
Public Relations Aids, Inc.
221 Park Ave. S.
New York, NY 10003

PR Calendar
Time & Life Bldg., Suite 4055
New York, NY 10020

PR Reporter
PR Publishing Co., Inc.
Box 600
Exeter, NH 03833

Print
RC Publications Inc.
6400 Goldsboro Rd. NW
Washington, DC 20034

Printing Impressions
North American Publishing Co.
2134 N. 13th St.
Philadelphia, PA 19107

Printing Magazine
466 Kinderkamack Rd.
Oradell, NJ 07649

Printing News
Printing News, Inc.
468 Park Ave. S.
New York, NY 10016

Printing Production
1213 W. Third St.
Cleveland, OH 44113

The Professional Photographer
PPA Publications and Events, Inc.
1090 Executive Way
Des Plaines, IL 60018

Public Relations Quarterly
44 W. Market St.
Rhinebeck, NY 12472

Public Relations Review
7338 Baltimore Blvd. #101A
College Park, MD 20740

Publicist
Public Relations Aids, Inc.
221 Park Ave. S.
New York, NY 10003

Publishers Weekly
R.R. Bowker Co.
Box 1807
Ann Arbor, MI 48106

Quorum Notes
IQ-International Quorum of
 Motion Picture Producers
PO Box 395
Oakton, VA 22124

Ragan Report
Lawrence Ragan Communica-
 tions, Inc.
407 S. Dearborn
Chicago, IL 60606

The Rangefinder
Rangefinder Publishing Co.
3511 Centinela Ave.
Los Angeles, CA 90066

SMPTE Journal
Society of Motion Picture & TV
 Engineers
862 Scarsdale Ave.
Scarsdale, NY 10583

Sales Training Magazine
Reinhardt/Keymer Publishing
60 E. 42nd St., Suite 1026
New York, NY 10017

Satellite Communications
Cardiff Publishing Corp.
3900 S. Wadsworth Blvd.
Denver, CO 80235

Satellite News
Phillips Publishing Inc.
7315 Wisconsin Ave.
Suite 1200 North
Bethesda, MD 20014

Science and Technology
48 E. 43rd. St., 4th Floor
New York, NY 10017

Shooting Commercials
Knowledge Industry Publications,
 Inc.
701 Westchester Ave.
White Plains, NY 10604

Show Business
Leo Shull Publications
136 W. 44th St.
New York, NY 10036

Sightlines
EFLA-Educational Film Library
 Association
17 W. 60th St.
New York, NY 10023

Studio Photography
PTN Publishing Corp.
250 Fulton Ave.
Hempstead, NY 11550

Successful Meetings Magazine
Bill Communications
1422 Chestnut St.
Philadelphia, PA 19102

Technical Photography
In-Plant Photography Inc.
250 Fulton Ave.
Hempstead, NY 11550

Television/Radio Age
Television Editorial Corp.
1270 Ave. of the Americas
New York, NY 10020

35mm Photography
Ziff-Davis Publishing Co.
One Park Ave.
New York, NY 10016

Training
Ziff-Davis Publishing Co.
One Park Ave.
New York, NY 10016

**Training and Development
Journal**
ASTD-American Society for
  Training and Development
Box 5307
Madison, WI 53705

Training Film Profiles
Olympic Media Information
71 W. 23rd St.
New York, NY 10010

**Training - The Magazine of
Human Resources Development**
Lakewood Publications
731 Hennepin Ave.
Minneapolis, MN 55403

Typographic
International Typographic Composition Association
2233 Wisconsin Ave. NW
Washington, DC 20007

Upper & Lower Case
International Typeface Corp.
216 E. 45th St.
New York, NY 10017

Variety
Variety, Inc.
154 W. 46th St.
New York, NY 10036

Video News
Phillips Publishing Inc.
7315 Wisconsin Ave.
Suite 1200 North
Bethesda, MD 20014

Video Systems
Intertec Publishing Corp.
9221 Quivira Rd.
PO Box 12901
Overland Park, KS 66212

Video Trade News
C.S. Tepfer Publishing Co.
PO Box 565
Ridgefield, CT 06877

Video User
Knowledge Industry Publications,
  Inc.
701 Westchester Ave.
White Plains, NY 10604

Videography
United Business Publications Inc.
475 Park Ave. S.
New York, NY 10016

View Magazine
Macro Communications
150 E. 58th St.
New York, NY 10022

Appendix IV: Major Colleges & Universities

Arizona State University
College of Fine Arts
Tempe, AZ 85281
Courses offered: technical course in graphic communications, design, print education.

Art Center, College of Design
1700 Lida St.
Pasadena, CA 91103
Courses offered: communications, design, film, illustration, photography.

Boston State College
Instructional Media Program
625 Huntington Ave.
Boston, MA 02115
Courses offered: instructional media, TV study (production, educational).

Boston University
School of Public Communications
640 Commonwealth Ave.
Boston, MA 02215
Courses offered: broadcast journalism, film, public relations, science communication, mass communications.

School of Visual Arts
640 Commonwealth Ave.
Boston, MA 02215
Courses offered: printing-related communication design, photography.

City University of New York, Brooklyn College
Film Program, School of Humanities
Bedford Ave. and Ave. H
Brooklyn, NY 11210
Courses offered: film.

Television/Radio Department
Bedford Ave. and Ave. H
Brooklyn, NY 11210
Courses offered: television/radio production (educational, commercial).

California College of Arts and Crafts
Division of Design
5212 Broadway
Oakland, CA 94618
Courses offered: general design, graphic design & illustration, environmental design.

This information is derived primarily from *The American Film Institute Guide to College Courses in Film and TV*, edited by Peter Bukalski (Princeton, NJ: Peterson's Guides, 1978) and *Peterson's Annual Guide to Graduate Study, Book II*, edited by Karen C. Hegener (Princeton, NJ: Peterson's Guides, 1980). Used with permission.

California Polytechnic State University
School of Applied Art & Design
San Luis Obispo, CA 93407
Courses offered: graphic communications (management orientation), printing technology and science.

California State University, Fresno
Department of Radio-TV-Cinema
Cedar and Shaw Aves.
Fresno, CA 93740
Courses offered: radio, TV, film, mass communications, education/instructional technical media, etc.

Carnegie Mellon University
Department of Art
Schenley Park
Pittsburgh, PA 15213
Courses offered: graphic arts (technical/management orientation), design, print.

Columbia University
Graduate School of Journalism
709 Journalism
New York, NY 10027
Courses offered: print and broadcast news media, information programs in government, industry and non-profit organizations.

Film Division - School of the Arts
513 Dodge Hall
New York, NY 10027
Courses offered: film production/criticism.

Teachers College
Curriculum and Teaching/Educational Technology and Media Department
New York, NY 10027
Courses offered: educational technology, educational media, instructional technology.

Cooper Union School of Art & Architecture
4 Cooper Square
New York, NY 10003
Courses offered: printing-related graphic design.

Cornell University
Communications Arts Graduate Center
640 Stewart Ave.
Ithaca, NY 14850
Courses offered: communications (in nutrition, agriculture, business), video.

Drake University
College of Fine Arts
25th St.
Des Moines, IA 50311
Courses offered: graphic design, commercial art.

East Texas State University
Department of Journalism and Graphic Arts
Commerce, TX 75428
Courses offered: journalism (news/editorial), advertising, public relations, photography.

194

Fairfield University
Graduate School of Corporate &
  Political Communication
Fairfield, CT 06430
*Courses offered: communications,
professional writing, video.*

Fordham University
East Fordham Rd.
Bronx, NY 10458
*Courses offered: communications
(news/information, media meth-
ods, media management, etc.).*

Germain School of Photography
Communication Dept.
225 Broadway
New York, NY 10007
*Courses offered: basic video tech-
niques, animation, motion picture
photography.*

Indiana University, Bloomington
Telecommunications Dept.
Radio and TV Center
College of Arts and Sciences
Bloomington, IN 47401
*Courses offered: telecommunica-
tions, mass communications, film-
making, TV production law, pub-
lic policy.*

Institute of Audio Research
64 University Place
New York, NY 10003
*Courses offered: music (in con-
junction with NYU School of
Music), multitrack recording technology.*

Jersey City State College
Media Arts Dept.
2039 Kennedy Blvd.
Jersey City, NJ 07305
*Courses offered: film, TV (educa-
tional, public service, etc.).*

Kansas City Art Institute
Dept. of Design
4415 Warwick Blvd.
Kansas City, MO 64111
*Courses offered: graphics, com-
munications, photography.*

Kent State University
School of Art, Division of Design
  and Illustration
Kent, OH 44242
*Courses offered: GLYPHIX (spe-
cial internship program which
functions as a professional studio).*

Kutztown State College
Kutztown, PA 19530
*Courses offered: corporate video
workshops.*

**Maryland College of Art and
Design**
10500 Georgia Ave.
Silver Spring, MD 20902
*Courses offered: design, visual
communications.*

Montclair State College
Speech and Theatre Dept.
Valley Road and Normal Ave.
Upper Montclair, NJ 07043
*Courses offered: broadcasting,
public media arts, TV.*

Fine Arts Dept.
School of Fine and Performing
    Arts
Valley Rd.
Upper Montclair, NJ 07043
*Courses offered: fine arts, film,
TV.*

New School for Social Research
Dept. of Cinematic Arts and TV
Visual Communications Division
66 W. 12th St.
New York, NY 10011
*Courses offered: film, production
techniques, video (workshops).*

Graduate Media Studies Program
66 Fifth Ave.
New York, NY 10011
*Courses offered: filmmaking (nar-
rative, animated, experimental)
TV (production, management,
industry training, news/documen-
tary, educational, experimental).*

New York Institute of Technology
Old Westbury Campus
Wheatly Rd.
Old Westbury, NY 11568
See New York Campus listing.

New York Campus
1855 Broadway
New York, NY 10023
*Courses offered: film (production,
appreciation, educational media/
instructional technology), TV
(production, educational, management).*

New York University
Dept. of Cinema Studies
School of the Arts
51 W. Fourth St.
New York, NY 10003
*Courses offered: history and criti-
cism of film, film theory, film
aesthetics.*

Division of Liberal Studies
School of Continuing Education
2 University Place, Room 21
New York, NY 10003
*Courses offered: scriptwriting,
audiovisual systems and techniques, film production.*

Undergraduate Institute of Film
    and TV and Graduate Institute
of Film and TV
40 E. 7th St.
New York, NY 10003
*Courses offered: film, TV (pro-
duction techniques, workshops).*

Parsons School of Design
66 W. 12th St.
New York, NY 10011
*Courses offered: all aspects of
design and environment (in conjunction with New School for
Social Research).*

Pratt Institute
School of Art and Design
Brooklyn, NY 11205
*Courses offered: communications
design, photography.*

Rensselaer Polytechnic Institute
Language, Literature, Communication and Rhetoric
Troy, NY 12181
*Courses offered: technical writing,
communication, (government, industry, education, journalism).*

Rhode Island School of Design
Division of Design
2 College St.
Providence, RI 02903
*Courses offered: graphic design,
photography, film, illustration,
television, printing.*

Rochester Institute of Technology
College of Fine & Applied Arts
One Lomb Memorial Dr.
Rochester, NY 14523
*Courses offered: communication
design & design application, gra-
phic arts, photography.*

San Diego State University
Telecommunication & Film Dept.
College Ave.
San Diego, CA 92182
*Courses offered: broadcast/film
(production, appreciation, relation-
ship to other media, educational).*

**School of the Art Institute of
Chicago**
Filmmaking Dept.
Columbus Dr. at Jackson Blvd.
Chicago, IL 60603
*Courses offered: film, TV, video
(2 way communications).*

**School of the Museum of Fine
Arts**
Boston, MA 02215
Courses offered: photography.

The School of Visual Arts
Film School
209 E. 23rd St.
New York, NY 10010
*Courses offered: Film, film pro-
duction, TV production, commercial photography, graphic design.*

**Southern Connecticut State
College**
Speech/Communication Dept.
501 Crescent St.
New Haven, CT 06515
*Courses offered: corporate video/
communications, interpersonal
communications industrial TV,
graphics, writing.*

Stanford University
Communication Dept.
Redwood Hall
Stanford, CA 94305
*Courses offered: film production,
broadcast management, news (in-
cludes educational TV study).*

**State University of New York at
Buffalo**
Art and Art History Dept.
3435 Main St.
Buffalo, NY 14214
*Courses offered: communication
design.*

Syracuse University
College of Visual and Performing
Arts
Syracuse, NY 13210
*Courses offered: film drama, film
art.*

S.I. Newhouse School of Public
Communications
Television-Radio-Film Dept.
215 University Place
Syracuse, NY 13210
*Courses offered: film, TV, radio
broadcast journalism, advertising,
communications photography,
educational communications, public relations communications, telecommunications, media administration.*

Temple University
School of Communications and
    Theatre
Philadelphia, PA 19122
*Courses offered: communications,
radio, television, film, journalism,
broadcast journalism, media administration, film or television
studies, organization communications, media law and ethics.*

Texas Tech University
Dept. of Art
Lubbock, TX 79409
*Courses offered: communication
design, film, TV.*

Dept. of Mass Communications
Lubbock, TX 79409
*Courses offered: noncommercial
telecommunications, educational
media, instructional technology.*

University of Alabama
School of Communication
PO Box 1482
University, AL 35486
*Courses offered: advertising/pub-
lic relations, broadcast and film
communication, journalism.*

**University of California, Los
Angeles**
Theatre Arts Dept.
405 Hilgard Ave.
Los Angeles, CA 90024
*Courses offered: production, writ-
ing, critical studies.*

University of Iowa
Division of Broadcasting and Film
Dept. of Speech and Dramatic Art
Iowa City, IA 52242
*Courses offered: broadcasting,
film.*

University of Michigan
Interdepartmental Doctoral Pro-
    gram in Mass Communication
Dept. of Communication
2040 LSA Building
Ann Arbor, MI 48109
*Courses offered: communication
theory and research (business,
government).*

**University of Minnesota, Minnea-
polis/St. Paul**
Speech Communication Dept.
Folwell Hall
Minneapolis, MN 55455
*Courses offered: broadcasting,
production, international broad-
casting and research.*

School of Journalism and Mass
    Communications
111 Murphy Hall
206 Church St.
Minneapolis, MN 55455
*Courses offered: photographic
communication (emphasis in film),
broadcast journalism.*

College of Education
Instructional Systems Labora-
    tories
178 Pillsbury Dr.
Minneapolis, MN 55455
*Courses offered: education (em-
phasis in TV).*

University of Pennsylvania
Annenberg School of Communi-
    cations
Philadelphia, PA 19104
*Courses offered: all aspects of
communications (emphasis in
codes and modes of communications, behavior of communicators
and interpreters and the nature of
the interactions between them,
communications systems and institutions).*

**Virginia Commonwealth Univers-
ity**
Communication Arts & Design
325 North Harrison St.
Richmond, VA 23284
*Courses offered: graphics, graphic
design typographics, illustration,
print production, video art, media
synthesis.*

**William Paterson College of New
Jersey**
Pompton Rd.
Wayne, NJ 07470
*Courses offered: radio, TV, jour-
nalism.*

Appendix V: Competitions

Aiken International Color Slide Exhibition
Aiken Camera Club
A.J. Hill Jr., Chairman
PO Box 782
Aiken, SC 29801
Date: October
Entry by September 6
Media: Slide
Category: Open

AMI Awards Festival and Competition
Association for Multi-Image
947 Old York Rd.
Abington, PA 19001
Date: End of October/November
Entry by September 5
Media: 2 projectors, 3-5 projectors, 6-8 projectors, 9-14 projectors, 15 or more projectors.
Categories: Commercial, non-commercial.

American Film Festival
EFLA - Educational Film Library
  Association
43 W. 61st St.
New York, NY 10023
Date: May
Entry by January 16; films in by February 13
Media: Film (16mm)
Categories: Training, technology, travel, health education, professional medical.

Art Directors Club Annual Exhibition
Arnie Arlow, Chairman
488 Madison Ave.
New York, NY 10022
Date: Spring
Entry by December 23
Media: Film (16mm), photography (advertising monochrome)
Categories: Industrial/education, promotional film, public service.

ASIFA East Animated Film Awards
International Animated Film
  Ass'n.
25 W. 43rd St., Room 1018
New York, NY 10036
Date: January 26
Entry by January 3
Media: Film (16mm) animated
Categories: Animated, direction, design, concept, sound track.

Athens International Film Festival
Giulio Scalinger, Director
PO Box 388
Athens, OH 43204
Date: April 21-30
Entry by April 3
Media: Film (16mm)
Categories: Feature films, animation, experimental, documentary, educational/promotional, social/political.

This information is derived primarily from *Gadney's Guide to 1800 International Contests, Festivals and Grants*, by Alan Gadney (Glendale, CA: Festival Publications, 1978). Used with permission.

Birmingham International Educational Film Festival
c/o Alabama Power Co.
PO Box 2641
Birmingham, AL 35291
Date: March-April
Entry by February 6
Media: Film (16mm), video tape
Categories: energy, corporate communications, public information: Video tape: Documentary, non-documentary.

Budapest Festival of Technical Films
Hungarian Optical, Acoustical, and Film Technical Society
Mrs. V. Vadasz, Secretary
VI Anker Koz 1
H-1061 Budapest, Hungary
Date: March
Entry by September 30
Media: 35mm, 16mm, super 8mm film
Categories: Information, industry, building/construction, telecommunication, traffic/transport.

Chicago 80
54 East Erie St.
Chicago, IL 60611
Date: Summer
Entry by March 15
Media: Film, video tape (¾"), filmstrip/slide film, photography.
Categories: Film, video tape: public relations, sales promotion, internal, educational, not-for-profit public services. Filmstrip/slide film: corporate (internal/external). Photography: Advertising, business journalism.

Chicago International Film Festival - Intercom Industrial Film and Videotape Competition
415 North Dearborn St.
Chicago, IL 60610
Date: September
Festival in November
Entry by July 25
Media: Video tape (¾"), film (70mm, 35mm, 16mm)
Categories: Business/industrial, training, health/medicine/safety.

Cine Golden Eagle Film Awards
Council on International Non-theatrical Events
1201 Sixteenth St. NW
Washington, DC 20036
Date: November
Entry by February 1 or August 15
Media: Film (35mm, 16mm, super 8mm, 8mm)
Categories: Industry/commerce, technology, medicine/dental.

Columbus International Film Festival
Columbus Film Council
8 East Broad St., Suite 706
Columbus, OH 43215
Date: October
Entry by July 10
Media: Film (16mm)
Categories: Business/industry, economics, employee relations, fund raising, industrial safety, manufacturing/technical, public relations, personnel/sales training, sales promotion.

Creativity Awards Show
Art Direction Magazine
19 W. 44th St.
New York, NY 10036
Date: November
Entry by June 10
*Media: Film (16mm), video tape
(¾" cassette), photographs (35mm
slides or photos).*
*Categories: 25 in graphics com-
munications.*

**Forox Corporation Creative Slide-
making Contest**
Forox Corporation
393 W. Ave.
Stamford, CT 06902
Date: November
Entry by September 30
Media: Slide
*Categories: Splits, zooms, neon
posturization. Open only to Forox
customers.*

**Gold Mercury International Film
Prize**
Venice Chamber of Commerce
Giovanni Giavi, President
S. Marco 2032
30124 Venice, Italy
Date: October
Entry by June 30
Media: Film (35mm, 16mm)
*Categories: Economic, documen-
tary industry, professional higher
training, public relations, trade/
distribution.*

Great Lakes Film Festival
PO Box 11583
Milwaukee, WI 53211
Date: April
Entry by February 20
Media: Film (16mm, super 8mm)
*Categories: Sponsored (industrial
product, educational).*
Open to midwest U.S.

**Greater Miami International Film
Festival (Festival of the Americas)**
J. Hunter Todd, Executive Direc-
tor
PO Box 01-4861 Flager
Miami, FL 33101
Date: November
Entry by September 20
*Media: Film (70mm, 65mm,
35mm, 16mm)*
*Categories: Business/industry, in-
house production, public relations,
recruiting, sales/marketing.*

IFPA Cindy Competition
Information Film Producers
Association
Mike Conaway, Director
3518 Cahuenga Blvd., W.
Suite 313
Hollywood, CA 90068
Date: September
Entry by May 1
*Media: Film (16mm), video (¾"),
filmstrips/slide films (35mm)*
*Categories: Informational, busi-
ness/industry/government, safety,
public relations, sales/marketing,
health, education.*

IMS Film and Videotape Competition
Industrial Management Society
Edward J. Kolod, Film Library
  Director
570 Northwest Highway
Des Plaines, IL 60016
Date: November
Entry by September 1
Media: Film (16mm), video
Categories: Industrial manage-
ment, management motivation,
management techniques, methods
improvement, industrial engineer-
ing, hospital management, work
performance rating.

Industrial Photography Indy Film Competition
Industrial Photography
475 Park Ave. S.
New York, NY 10016
Date: September
Entry by April 15
Media: Industrial film
Categories: Advertising/sales,
training/education/employee re-
lations, public relations, short-
shorts. Open to in-house film
makers.

Industrial Photography Photo Contest
Industrial Photography Magazine
475 Park Ave. S.
New York, NY 10016
Date: April
Entry by January 12
Media: Prints, slides
Category: Open to industrial photo-
graphers.

Industrial Photographic Dept.of the Year Award Competition
Professional Photographers of
  America
1090 Executive Way
Des Plaines, IL 60018
Date: July/August
Entry by June 1
Media: Photographic prints, film,
slides, transparencies, video tape,
engineering drawings, microfilm
techniques, etc.
Category: Industrial/business prob-
lem solving.

ITVA International Videotape Competition
International Television Ass'n.
136 Sherman Ave.
Berkeley Heights, NJ 07922
Date: March
Entry: January 12
Media: Video tape
Categories: Training, information,
sales/marketing, public service/
public relations, company news,
health and medicine, environment,
education.

International Film and TV Festival of New York
International F.T.F. Corporation
251 W. 57th St.
New York, NY 10019
Date: November
Entry by September 1
Media: Multimedia/mixed media,
filmstrips/slide program, film
(16mm), video tape (2" or cassette).
Categories: Corporate image, pub-
lic relations, services training,
manufacturing, product presenta-
tion.

International Multi-Image Festival - Vail, Colorado
Sylvia Allen
PO Box 272
Fairhaven, NJ 07701
Date: August
Entry by July 8
Media: 2-5 projectors, 6-11 projectors, 12 or more projectors.
Categories: Religious and spiritual education, entertainment, documentary, sales and marketing, meetings, motivation/recognition.

Long Island International Film Festival
James Arcuri, Founder/Director
244 Mineola Blvd.
Mineola, NY 11505
Date: December 18
Entry by December 2
Media: Film (35mm, 16mm)
Categories: Business/industrial, technical/research development, labor management, public relations, training, promotion, marketing, economics/finance.

National Committee on Films for Safety - Contest for Films on Safety NCFS
William E. Wendland, Secretary
444 North Michigan Ave.
27th floor
Chicago, IL 60611
Date: Spring
Entry by January 30
Media: Film (16mm)
Categories: Traffic/transport, home, recreation, sports, instructional, inspirational, documentary.

National Educational Film Festival
Montera Educational Film Foundation
Carol Howe
5555 Ascot Dr.
Oakland, CA 94611
Date: April-May
Entry by March 10
Media: Film (16mm), filmstrips/slide show (35mm)
Categories: Educational, business/career/vocational guidance, health/hygiene/safety.

Nikon Photomicro/Macrography Contest
Nikon Instrument Division
Susie Weiss, Secretary
623 Stewart Ave.
Garden City, NY 11530
Date: Winter
Entry by September 30
Media: Slides (photomicrograph and photomacrograph color)
Category: Any subject and technique. Open to scientific photographers.

The One Show
Art Directors Club, Inc. and Copy Club
488 Madison Ave.
New York, NY 10022
Date: Spring
Entry by December 23
Media: Print, television commercials
Categories: Advertising, industrial, educational, promotional TV (broadcast).

Ottawa International Animated Film Festival - Canadian Film Institute
S. Wayne Clarkson, Director
75 Albert St., Suite 1105
Ottawa, Ontario KIP 5E7 Canada
Date: August
Entry by July 1
Media: Film (animated, 16mm, 35mm, 70mm)
Category: Promotional, instructional.

Public Relations Film Festival
Public Relations Society of
America
845 Third Ave.
New York, NY 10022
Date: November
Entry by June 30
Media: Film (16mm), video tape (¾" cassette)
Categories: Corporate identity, institutional identity, community relations, internal communications, public education, product exposure. Open to PRSA members.

San Francisco International Film Festival
Claude Jarman, Director
1409 Bush St.
San Francisco, CA 94109
Date: October
Entry by August 15
Media: Film (35mm, 16mm)
Categories: Nontheatrical, industry/business/government training, medical health, technical/scientific.

Sherman Fairchild Film Competition
75 Mall Dr.
Commack, NY 11725
Date: January
Entry by September 15
Media: Super 8mm, slide (35mm), 110mm filmstrip
Categories: Sales, point of purchase.

Type Directors Club Awards
12 East 42nd St.
New York, NY 10017
Date: May
Entry by beginning of February
Media: Calligraphy, lettering, metal and film typesetting
Categories: Brochure, advertisement, trademark, private press printing, and/or label.

U.S. Industrial Film Festival
United States Festivals
Association
J.W. Anderson, Chairman
1009 Bellwood
Bellwood, IL 60104
Date: May
Entry by March 1
Media: 16mm, 35mm filmstrips, 35mm slide programs, ¾" video
Categories: In-plant, government, advertising/sales, promotional, recruiting, employee communications, industrial/technical, medicine/health.

**Video Tape Production Associa-
tion Monitor Awards**
Videotape Production Association
63 West 83rd St.
New York, NY 10024
Date: May
Entry
Media: Video tape
*Categories: Non-broadcast pro-
grams, corporate communica-
tions, medical, education.*

Index

About the Author

Eugene Marlow has spent the last 15 years working in communications, first with the United States Air Force as an award-winning Vietnam War historian, then as news editor for a trade publication. For the last nine years he has managed communications functions and provided consulting services for a variety of organizations, including Citibank, Prudential Insurance and Union Carbide Corporation, where he is now Manager, Corporate Video/AV Communications.

Mr. Marlow has taught graduate courses in corporate communications at Fordham University. He has served as Director of Professional Development for the International Television Association (ITVA) and was founder and first chairman of its New York Chapter. He is currently Chairman of the Corporate Applications Panel of the American Video Institute, and a member of the Audiovisual Communications Committee of the Association of National Advertisers.

Mr. Marlow is a frequent guest speaker at professional organizations, trade shows and educational institutions. He was a contributing editor to *Videography* from 1976-1980. His first book, *Communications and the Corporation* (United Business Publications, Inc.), was published in 1978.

He is currently completing his Ph.D. in Media Ecology at New York University, and holds an MBA from Golden Gate College, San Francisco.

Mr. Marlow is an avid jazz composer and pianist. He lives with his wife, Judy, in New York City.